FALCONRY
AND BIRDS OF PREY
IN THE GULF

by David Remple
and Christian Gross

Published with the support
and encouragement of

Published by
Motivate Publishing

PO Box 2331
Dubai, UAE
Tel: (04) 824060
Fax: (04) 824436

PO Box 43072
Abu Dhabi, UAE
Tel: (02) 311666
Fax: (02) 311888

London House
26/40, Kensington High Street
London W8 4PF
Tel: (071) 938 2222
Fax: (071) 937 7293

Directors:
Obaid Humaid Al Tayer
Ian Fairservice

First published 1993

ISBN 1 873544 39 1

Printed by Emirates Printing Press, Dubai

British Library Cataloguing-in-Publication Data.
A catalogue record for this book is available
from the British Library.

FOREWORD

For nearly thirty years I have travelled, a pilgrimage, to fly falcons in the deserts of the Middle East with many Arab friends. From the Atlantic shores of North Africa to the desert fringes of India, we have found and hunted houbara bustard.

My early days in Abu Dhabi, where houbara were to be found in goodly numbers less than an hour's journey from the mud brick and *barasti* town, when we killed desert hares where the Abu Dhabi Hilton now stands, initiated me into the art and practice of desert hawking. How generously the men showed me their skills and taught me the detail of it all, yet were fascinated to know that we flew hawks in England and were equally keen to hear of what we flew our falcons: Were there houbara in our country?

Perhaps I got there just in time to still get a taste of what has been so well described in Wilfred Thesiger's great travel book, *Arabian Sands*. On one or two occasions we hunted from camels but already the Land Rover was making 'roads' across the sands, enabling us to hunt along the coast towards Dubai, or a day or two later to be searching for houbara under the frowning Jebel Hafit and from there hunting south or away towards the Liwa.

We usually took with us only four or five falcons, perhaps one Saker and the rest my favourite, the Peregrine, and would find sufficient houbara, with the occasional desert hare or stone curlew, to provide meat for our small evening meal. We travelled light, no tents, but slept about the camp fire with rifle and bandoleer handy beside our one or two blankets. The marvellous companions of those hunts I still value as special friends today.

Before very long, with increasing numbers of hawks to fly and houbara now thinner on the ground, hawking parties had to look further afield for 'pastures new', where houbara were to be found in undreamt of numbers. Well I remember my first visit to the deserts to central Pakistan in the late 1960s, a city of tents set out some hours' drive from the nearest town, a great gathering of falconers, drivers, servants, pots and Pakistanis together with such numbers of lovely Sakers and perfect Peregrines, and evening feasts on the very many houbara caught in the surrounding country.

Today, we still find houbara, both east and west, in sufficient numbers to try our falcons and to test their skill and bravery. However we now have modern technology to aid us. Tiny radio transmitters can be attached to the leg or the tail of a falcon to aid in finding her should she be lost. We also have the knowledge and expertise of specialist veterinary surgeons, such as my good friend Dr David Remple, to help us, and come to the rescue when our favourite falcon has 'bumblefoot' or '*jidrî*'.

Few books have been written in the past fifty years on Arab hawking and so we '*aficionados*' look forward with pleasure to any addition to the small but specialised library. Wilfred Thesiger, of course, reported on his experiences, hawking with HH Sheikh Zayed bin Sultan Al Nahyan about Buraimi in the late 1940s. Since then, other than articles in falconry magazines, only two books of note have been produced on the subject: *Falconry in Arabia* by Mark Allen, and the work in Arabic of Said Salmaan Abu Athra.

David Remple and Christian Gross make an important addition to this small but exclusive library, the more so in that this interesting book covers much that is new on the birds of prey that occur in the Gulf region, on flight, breeding and health.

Roger Upton

CONTENTS

A Falcon in the desert at sunset.

A Brief History of Falconry

by Cheryl J Remple

It is generally believed that falconry originated on the Central Asian plateaux, an area between current day Korea, Japan and China. While figures are unavailable, at different times this area holds one of the highest concentrations of birds of prey usable for falconry — Saker Falcons, Peregrine Falcons, Lanner Falcons and eagles. Legends of falconry expeditions by the Mongolian conqueror, Genghis Khan (c.1167-1227), tales of young princes being saved from starvation by sharing the quarry of a falcon, and the romantic hunting trips of knights in the Middle Ages, culminate to perpetuate an interest in the art of falconry.

The earliest record of falconry lives in the art of the Hittites, and dates back to the 13th century BC. There is little or no support in art or literature that falconry was practised in Egyptian, Greek or Roman civilisations, although all three revered the falcon for its powers. We do have from Khorsabad, Mesopotamia, an Assyrian scripture on the subject, which dates from approximately the 8th century BC. And an early treatise on falconry is attributed to Ctesias, court doctor to the Persian king, Artexeises II (Mnemon), in 416 BC.

Art and literature of Medieval Europe overflows with legends of falconry, and its importance is demonstrated by the code of laws, *Loi Gambette* (published in 50l AD) — which stated that someone convicted of hawk stealing had to pay a fine or with six ounces of his own flesh! However, monks begged for protection of their crops against hunting parties of knights. In 760 AD, Pepin the Short, king of the Franks, restricted falconry, and indeed Charlemagne, who ruled in the early 9th century AD, forbade serfs and churchmen from participating. Most ignored the decree. By 900 AD the 'Master

An historic photograph by Ronald Codrai of Sheikh Saeed, Ruler of Dubai 1912-58, with his falcons.

A detail from 'De Arte Venandi Cum Avibus', written between 1244 and 1250 by Frederick II.

of the Hawkes' had a social ranking 4th to the king of Wales. In *De Arte Venandi Cum Avibus,* which was written between 1244 and 1250 by Frederick II, it was declared that falconry was, "the noblest of all sports". According to old trade notes, two Gyrfalcons would buy a licence to export Linconshire corn to Norway, while in the 16th century, the Knights of Malta paid the Viceroy of Sicily rent of one falcon per year. In 1764 the Dukes of Atholl were granted feudal tenancy of the Isle of Man with payment of two white Gyrfalcons to be paid at coronation of each succeeding monarch. Inevitably falcons were used for barter, and as anything that can be bought eventually loses value, so did falcons. Due to increasing land pressures in Europe, falconry largely became the sole privilege of the gentry, and finally royalty. Conservation rested upon the bureaucratic concept of income and land holdings, defining resources available to the hunter and his falcon.

As the Renaissance spread across Europe during the 15th and 16th century, so did falconry. Flanders became the centre of falcon suppliers to all the courts of Europe, and so it remained in Valkensward, Holland until this century. King Louis XIII of France

had 140 falcons, organised with their falconers into six specialised groups according to quarry taken. His hunting manor built in 1642 was the embryo of Versailles. Tzar Alexis of Russia, enjoyed falconry on a grand scale — 3,000 birds all outfitted with bells of gold and silver and hoods covered in jewels. Samuel Pepys (a diarist writing in the mid-17th century) noted the arrival of the Russian Ambassador to London, with numerous attendants carrying hawks bedecked with ornate bejewelled gloves, hoods and bags as a state present for King Charles II of England.

After a century of active falconry, this situation soon changed. In 1748, King Louis XV of France was forced to abolish the Royal Falconry offices because of abuses and extravagances. The Royal Mews (from the French *muer,* to moult) in London, had already been converted to stables by 1537. Falconry flourished in Europe for more than 400 years, but the invention of firearms heralded its decline. Agricultural pressures from an expanding agrarian culture, the migration of rural populations with the rise of commerce and industry, wars and the inevitable depletion of quarry also assisted in its decline. Today the sport continues as an anachronism, although it is a shadow of its former glory.

In the isolation of the east, falconry developed separately from that in the west. The eastern spread of falconry is documented by the arrival in Japan, in 244 AD, of many trained Goshawks from China. The *Chronicle Nihonskoki* (written in circa 355 AD) notes the presentation of an unidentified bird to the Emperor — a visiting Korean was the only person who knew how to train the bird and as a consequence was placed in charge of a newly established 'hawk office' or 'takataibe' — at one time the takataibe was as important to the Japanese as their army and navy. Over time hawking parties grew and provided pleasure for the nobility, but they were also used to surreptitiously inspect landholdings and act as camouflage for war parties.

As hawking became more important to the fabric of Japanese society, so too did the need for husbandry to protect the quarry. Certain farms in each neighbourhood were chosen to protect game. In 1596, during the Japanese-Korean War, Koreans offered to trade hawks for food. This led to a healthy trade that lasted beyond the 16th-century war.

Falcon trading between Korea and Japan also led to the introduction of quarantine. A 13-day observation period was introduced and no building that housed a sick bird could be reused. Falconry declined with the introduction of firearms, the tastes of the times and the whims of rulers.

Poised on the brink of its greatest expansion, the spread of Islam (632-936) also brought a spread of falconry. The *Hadith* (collection of the Prophet Mohammed's sayings) records the conversion to Islam of the Prophet's uncle upon his return from hunting with his hawk. As further evidence we know the Umayyad Caliph of Damascas, 680-83 AD, Yazid bin Muawiyyah, ordered falconry hunting lodges to be built. These lodges were subsequently used by future Caliphs.

In the Jordanian desert at this time, we see a divergence in Arab falconry. Bedu continued their old ways, insulated by the isolation of the desert and the requirements of diet. Other Arabs were absorbing and modifying new techniques learned during their expansion through Persia and contact with different cultures. The first known Arabic treatise on falconry, *Kitab Manafi Al Tair* (*Book of the Benefits of Birds*) lists 153 chapters that deal with every aspect of the hawk, including their diseases. It was a compendium of the knowledge of the Persians, Turks and Indians, concentrating mostly on Goshawks. The preference for Goshawks coincides with their popularity in India, Korea, China and Japan and follows the trade routes through Central Asia. In *Falconry in Arabia*, Mark Allen suggests an interesting line of research: "The Goshawk as a vehicle of cultural pollination in medieval Asia." But the *Kitab Al Hayawan* (*Book of Animals*) by Al Jahiz (c.869) specifically notes that Arabs may not be seen carrying Goshawks but Peregrines and Sakers. The preference for these falcons continues today amongst conservatives who wish to pursue falconry as part of their cultural identity.

Falconry rose to esoteric heights with some Muslim (Persian, Iraqi and Syrian) falconers. They flew their hawks at ducks by moonlight and flew all kinds, sizes and sexes of raptors at diverse and challenging quarry.

There was a medieval Arabic biological system of classification of falcons based on colour and place of origin statistically supported by the huge numbers of falcons seen — experience not available to falconers today. This form of classification lingers today in the Arabian Gulf but distilled by time has lost its veracity.

It was between 1096 and 1204 that we see the mixing of Eastern and Western falconry. Indeed the Arabs introduced the hood and lure to European falconry. As in Europe, tales of knightly deeds exist in Arab literature. Saladin reportedly took pity on Richard the Lion-Hearted's falcons during the siege of the third Crusade and sent his best poultry to feed the starving birds. The contribution of Arab literature to the history of falconry seems to have declined with the Mongol invasion of Baghdad in 1258. Falconry declined in Arab lands dominated by the Ottoman Turks, Mongols and others; although, until recently, remained unchanged in the stronghold of the Arabian desert and Gulf region. The impetus of cars, radios, tracking telemetry and the evolution of falconry from sport to art is breathing new life into the ancient practices of the bedu...

It is the end of the day. Arabs are gathered around a fire and as the sun sets the call to prayer rings out across the desert from the nearby city. The talk is of past and present feats of their falcons; it is a time for poetry. They compare their birds against the legends of the past and against each other. They anticipate the hunting trips that will dominate the winter season. They enjoy coffee, *halwa* and camaraderie. Sheikhs, bedu and townsmen are gathered together in that circle to cement political, commercial and human bonds. It is a time of day when time stands still and falconry in the Gulf is caught in that timelessness.

HH Sheikh Zayed bin Sultan Al Nahyan's falconers, photographed by explorer Wilfred Thesiger in 1949.

FALCONRY IN THE ARABIAN GULF

The main falconry region of Arabia lies within the Arabian Gulf region of the peninsula and extends well into the interior of Saudi Arabia. Specifically, it extends from the United Arab Emirates in the southern Gulf, northward through Qatar and Bahrain into Kuwait. Its southern limits extend from the northern edge of the Empty Quarter to Medina. The region becomes patchy and gradually diminishes in the north toward Iraq. Only little known and scattered pockets still exist in and around Syria and Jordan. Falconry is not practised in Oman and the Yemen.

Before examining falconry in the Arabian Gulf region, or the practice of falconry anywhere in the world, for that matter, it is important to realise that the techniques and methods of the practice are dictated and limited by the terrain, climate and biota of the geographical region, and these in turn are modified by the culture and traditions of the people. The limiting variables are climate, topography, floral density (protective cover for prey species), locally available raptors and local quarry that the raptors are willing or able to catch. Once these limits define what can be done, cultural values and tradition shape exactly how it is done. The limiting variables of the Arabian Gulf region have established a rather specialised form of falconry, which can be considered by the remainder of the world as 'uniquely Arab'.

Much of Arab falconry remains cloaked in mystery as the Gulf Arabs have left little written record of their practice. The bulk of written information on falconry centres around western falconry. Therefore, to attempt a description of Arab falconry to a reader unfamiliar with falconry in general, is difficult and often necessitates

Hooded falcons outside a hunting tent.

11

comparisons to the overall scope of the practice. Throughout most of the world falconry blossomed in ancient times. It began as a means of supplementing man's diet with meat that was more efficiently obtained with the use of raptors, than by other methods (snares, spears, arrows, etc.). However, in the West, which was so much richer than the desert in both the quantity and variety of what we now refer to as recreational game species, falconry gradually evolved from a food gathering means into a highly refined art form known as the 'gentleman's sport'.

Within the last century the motivation to become a falconer focused less on obtaining meat for the table and more on becoming a participant in Nature's great drama of the chase, without any risk to oneself, and to be able to summon at will the exciting spectacle of raptor chasing quarry. The most taxing flights possible were often intentionally created, and the emphasis was directed away from the size (in terms of numbers) of the kill and more on sport and the quality of the flight. With the introduction of firearms in the 17th century, falconry declined. However, throughout much of the period following the introduction of firearms, falconry was continued by tiny groups of dedicated practitioners, motivated strictly by a shared passion for the 'ultimate hunting sport'. Now there appears to be a resurgence of interest, and in the west, falconry is making a comeback.

Historically, Arabia presented a different situation — the forces that effected change nearly everywhere else could not penetrate the geographical isolation of the desert or break a resistance to change demonstrated by the people. Hunting for the desert nomad was strictly pragmatic. Herd stock was generally protected for the milk that was obtained from it, and meat was the reward of a successful hunt. Although hunting with falcons provided great enjoyment, the main impetus for doing it was to supplement the nomad's diet. Survivalist techniques dictated that the value of food obtained by hunting must not outweigh the effort expended in catching it. Mark Allen illustrates the point succinctly in *Falconry in Arabia*: "The desert nomad clearly flew his falcons because he wanted to hunt and eat; he did not go hunting because he wanted to see his falcons fly." This is an important distinction to bear in mind, because it contrasts the values of Western and Arabian falconry and highlights their differences.

Now, the world's dependence on oil has created an inevitable commingling with the outside world, and the old barriers to change have begun to crumble. Remote tribal settlements have been buried under bustling modern cities. Yet out of the wake of this explosive change the Arabs have seen an even greater need to preserve a part of their heritage. Falconry is an example. It remains a major link to the nomadic past, and reminds the Arabs of their ties to the desert. For this reason it has remained largely unchanged in its practice and methodology during the past one thousand years. However, the conveniences and luxuries that wealth has introduced are proving too valuable to resist. Changes are gradually creeping into the old ways.

Quarry of Arabian falconry

The words 'quarry' and 'prey' are often used interchangeably by falconers. To avoid confusion, prey specifically refers to those species that a predator normally catches, and feeds upon for its own survival. Quarry, more correctly, refers to species that are pursued by the raptors of falconry.

The objective of falconry is to hunt and catch quarry with trained raptors, usually falcons. The

The handsome Chestnut-bellied Sandgrouse is rarely captured by a falcon as it is an extremely fast flyer.

The highly camouflaged Houbara is usually seen only after it has been startled out from its sleeping place.

falcon must be rewarded when her efforts are successful; therefore, she is usually allowed to eat a portion of the quarry she has caught, while the remainder is usually retained by the falconer. Diverse habitat such as mountain and foothill areas, wadis, oases, coastal areas or merely simple watering holes all provide a diversity of resident quarry that falcons could potentially be flown against. In the United Arab Emirates the **Collared Dove** (*Streptopelia decaocto*), **Turtle Dove** (*Streptopelia turtur*), **Palm Dove** (*Streptopelia senegalensis*), **Rock Dove** (Columbia livia), **Quail** (*Coturnix coturnix*), **Sand Partridge** (*Ammoperdix heyi*), **Grey Francolin** (*Francolinus pondicerianus*), **Chukar** (*Alectoris chukar*) and **Chestnut-bellied Sandgrouse** (*Pterocles exustus*) all exist in scattered abundance, and all could be potential quarry for falconry.

However, the inhibiting force of local tradition and the limitation of bedu training techniques have excluded these species as quarry for Arab style falconry. A few isolated cases exist where sandgrouse have been taken by falcons, but most of those instances were 'lucky accidents', as sandgrouse are considered, and rightfully so, too fast to be taken with falcons flown straight from the hand. Others such as partridges and doves are either protected by law or simply not considered worth the effort.

There are only three species that traditionally are pursued by Arab falconers. All are 'catchable' by falcons flown straight from the hand and all offer the bonus of meat for the cooking pot. They are the Houbara Bustard, the Stone Curlew and Arabian hare.

Houbara Bustard
(*Clamydotis undulata macqueenii*)

The one entity, more than any other limiting factor that has influenced, but more specifically, defined and moulded the way Arab falconry has evolved and continues to be practised, is the **Houbara** or **Macqueen's Bustard** (*Chlamydotis undulata macqueenii*). Known simply as the 'Houbara' this relentlessly sought-after quarry forms the virtual core of Arab falconry, and all falconry methodology and tradition revolve around its pursuit.

The Houbara Bustard prefers harsh, arid plains with little cover except scattered shrubs. An omnivorous bird, it exists on a variety of desert plants and insects. The bird nests from Egypt to outer Mongolia, and migrates into Arabia, Iran,

13

Stone Curlew are often seen in small groups. With care, a single curlew can be herded away and flushed into flight without disturbing the others.

Pakistan and India from late November until March. In the winter feeding areas shoots of shrubby, aromatic plants and grubs are the preferred food items. Small lizards and mammals occasionally supplement their diet. Much of the migratory travelling and feeding is done at night.

Well-adapted to the desert, the bird is superbly camouflaged against any sandy backdrop. Crouching motionless near a shrub, the Houbara is undetectable to the inexperienced eye. When foraging for food, Houbara prefer to search on foot rather than fly, even when large distances separate edible items. This foraging habit leaves tracks in the early morning, dew-laden sand, and the tracks are usually the only real evidence of a Houbara in the area. The Houbara feeds singly or in small groups, and nowhere within its wintering range can it ever be considered common.

Yet as difficult and time-consuming as they are to locate, their size and the delectability of their meat makes it all worth while for the Arab falconer. Houbaras are related to cranes, and the Houbaras of the Arabian Gulf region are typically crane-shaped. As a falcon must be fed from the prey she catches — to maintain her interest — the Houbara again, is the ideal quarry. Large males can weigh over three kilograms and large females over two kilograms. Therefore, a single catch usually feeds several people, and rewards the falcon for her efforts. A successful day's catch of several Houbara provides a veritable feast for the hunting party and reaffirms the bonds of the Arab falconer to the desert.

Stone Curlew (*Burbinus oedicnemus*)

Arab falconers refer to the Stone Curlew as 'Kairowan'. When pursued with falcons, the Kairowan arouses almost as much excitement and passion as the Houbara Bustard. However, due to the size of the Houbara, the importance of the Kairowan, as a quarry of Arab falconry, is greatly overshadowed.

The Kairowan has flight characteristics and feeding habits similar to the Houbara; and therefore, is caught by the use of the same falconry techniques and methods used to catch Houbara. Additionally, those that are caught go into the cooking pot, the same as Houbara. But unlike the Houbara, Stone Curlews are related to plovers; therefore, they are typically plover-sized birds, and as such their importance as food quarry is greatly diminished.

English-speaking people refer to the Stone Curlew as a 'Thick-knee', because of its conspicuously long, yellow legs and prominent 'knees' (the reference is actually to the ankle joints). This bird has a relatively large head and conspicuously large, strikingly yellow eyes. The body size of a female approximates that of a large pigeon, while males have a body size similar to a partridge.

The Kairowan make a brief migratory appearance in the Gulf on the way to and from their wintering grounds to the south. The first appearance is from October to approximately mid-December. The second appearance is from early February until the end of March. Much like the Houbara, Kairowan prefer to migrate at night and their feeding habits tend to be even more nocturnal than those of the Houbara. Once having arrived in an area, food is mostly sought out on foot. Their diet consists of insects, plant shoots and small reptiles. Unlike Houbara, Stone Curlew are vocal when they arrive at a night feeding area. Their plover-like "Kleee-Kleeeuuu" often alerts camping falconers to their location — where they will be found sleeping during the day.

Arabian hare (*Lepus capensis*)

The Arabian hare is a much smaller version of the European hare. They are only about one third the size of the European, and most weigh approximately 1.5 kilograms. One ecological principle states northern species tend to be larger than their tropical counterparts. Another principle states the appendages (such as ears) tend to be proportionally larger in tropical species than in northern species. This desert hare adheres to both principles. The ears are strikingly large, and they are thought to act as 'radiators' to help rid the body of excess heat. Like the Houbara and Kairowan, the hare is largely nocturnal in its feeding habits. Much of their day is spent crouched under a bush or rock to avoid the heat.

In the United Arab Emirates the hare was nearly hunted to extinction with firearms. Consequently, the hunting of this species was wisely banned to allow it to make a comeback, and thankfully it now appears to be increasing in numbers again.

Arab falconers refer to the desert hare as 'arnab'. The Empty Quarter of Saudi Arabia still offers the Arab falconer a chance to chase this 'zig-zagging' arnab around bushes and over dunes with his falcon. As the hind legs of the hare can kick with some ferocity, feathers are often broken in the ensuing ground tussle. For this reason hare hunting is sometimes delayed until the end of the Houbara and Kairowan season. Saker Falcons are best flown at this quarry, as Peregrines are normally loathe to engage in a ground tussle, especially with something that kicks!

The hunting of hares with falcons is still permitted in the Empty Quarter of Saudi Arabia.

Traditional birds of Arab falconry

Arab falconers classify and name falcons in their own way, but their system conflicts with western terminology. For clarification it is necessary, once again, to examine the situations and conditions surrounding desert falconry. In western countries and throughout Asia, falconers have always had the choice of being able to acquire a raptor either as a nestling or as a wild-caught, fully grown, experienced hunter. In western terminology a raptor that is taken from a nest before it is able to fly is known as an 'eyass'. (Note that a raptor's nest is called an eyrie) A raptor that is trapped shortly after it leaves the eyrie, but before it embarks on its first migratory journey, is known as a 'soar hawk'. A raptor that is trapped in the autumn, usually on migration and in juvenile plumage, is referred to as a 'passager' or 'passage falcon' (or 'passage hawk', depending on the species). A wild-caught raptor in adult plumage is known as a 'haggard'.

Each category has its merits and drawbacks. The positive side of the eyass highlights tameness and manageability; the negative side is that it has no experience whatsoever as a hunter. A fledgling raptor must be taught how to hunt by its parents; therefore, if man should intervene before the raptor's education is complete, he must assume the parental responsibility. Since man cannot fly, education must be completed through many trial and error situations. The process requires time and patience. However, the inexperience of the eyass establishes a certain dependency on its 'new parent' which makes it less likely to fly away and be lost.

The haggard on the other hand, though a superb and knowledgeable hunter, tends to be independent, ill-tempered and difficult to tame. The haggard is a hardened survivor — it has graduated from being a reckless teenager and survived the many life-threatening situations that target the young and inexperienced. But its removal from the wild is most likely to result in the removal of an established member of the breeding population, and this has a negative impact on the overall population.

The characteristics of the passager consist of a blend of the best features of the eyass and the haggard, with little of the less desirable features of each. The passage falcon exhibits the tameness and manageability approaching that of the eyass, and adds the attributes of superb physical conditioning and the seasoned hunting experience of the haggard. The only fault of the passage falcon, indeed if it can be called a fault, stems from her

Saker Falcons come in a variety of colour phases. This large adult displays the blond ('Ashgar') phase, most valued of the 'typical' Sakers.

An immature Peregrine Falcon.

relative lack of fear; and that is that she tends to be over-zealous and reckless in her pursuit of quarry. Also, from an ecological standpoint, statistics have shown that nearly three of every four falcons born do not survive to see their second year of life. Competition between peers, the acquisition of hunting expertise and juvenile disease all threaten a raptor during the early years of life. Therefore, removal from the wild population of a juvenile falcon, in its first year of life, has very little impact on the overall population.

Raptors that are suitable for Arab falconry do not breed in the Arabian Gulf region. Those that do breed have consequently gone unnoticed or have not been acknowledged. Therefore, the heritage of Arab falconry does not include a knowledge of eyasses or their training, and there are no equivalent words in the Arabic vocabulary for eyass or soar hawk.

Arab falconers refer to falcons in juvenile plumage as 'farkh' and to those in adult plumage as 'jernass'. Most farkh falcons will be passagers except for the occasional resident Barbary or Lanner Falcon that may be trapped in the vicinity of its nest. A jernass can be a wild-caught falcon in adult plumage, or simply one that shows major evidence of adult plumage. For example, Peregrines are notoriously poor moulters, and some captive falcons may only undergo a partial moult in their first year, while retaining much of their juvenile plumage. Since jernass properly refers more to age than plumage, any falcon that can be assumed to be older than one year, regardless of its plumage, is jernass.

Since most Arabs have not witnessed raptors breeding in a natural state, they have not seen the size difference between males and females. Because these differences are great, the assumption has been made that the male and female probably constitute two separate species. Furthermore, it has been mistakenly assumed that the males are larger and stronger than the females (refer to the discussion of reversed sexual dimorphism (RSD) in chapter four). For these reasons we see the large females being assigned masculine Arabic names and the smaller males being assigned feminine names.

Only falcons are used in Gulf Arab falconry. The limitless expanse of the desert, its relative lack of protective cover and the demanding, long-range flight of quarry such as the Houbara Bustard and Stone Curlew, all clearly favour the use of falcons.

The size of Houbara necessitates the use of large falcons, and the evasive flight tactics employed by the Houbara, necessitates the use of hearty falcons with 'staying power'. Once a Houbara has taken flight, it presents a challenge to the falcon's endurance. A healthy, well muscled falcon going all out can initially 'close the gap', but she expends great effort and energy in doing so. The ultra-light wing-loaded Houbara, with her gull-like manoeuvrability and razor-sharp turning ability, usually escapes the initial closing efforts of the falcon. At just about the time a falcon attempts to grab a Houbara in flight, she will suddenly find herself going in the opposite direction of her intended meal! These initial 'empty-handed' efforts place a large demand on her patience and physical fitness. A good falcon that persists will be rewarded, but only if she has the staying power to exhaust and intimidate the Houbara.

Only the large, powerful falcon has the necessary ingredients required to catch and hold Houbara on a regular basis, and these are the Saker and the Peregrine. In the West and throughout Asia, falcons, accipitrine hawks and eagles have all been employed in falconry. The question is often asked, "Why don't the Arabs use goshawks ('baz' as Arab and Indian falconers refer to them) for catching Houbara?" — since they possess the size, strength, courage and even greater acceleration and turning ability than falcons. The answer is simple; goshawks lack the endurance necessary for the long chase.

The Saker Falcon is clearly the favourite among Arab falconers. Sakers vary greatly in size (within the same sex), feather marking pattern and plumage coloration. Colour hues range from 'blond' (light brown marking on a cream background) to yellowish and reddish and from rich chocolate-brown to slate-grey. The ashgar colour morph (blond) is the most highly valued among the 'typical' Sakers. 'Tibri' is the term assigned to those of a yellowish or golden hue. 'Ahmar' pertains to the Sakers with a reddish hue to their backs and tails, and 'adham' is a morph tending toward dull brown or grey. 'Akdhar' is what Arab falconers refer to as a 'green' hue colour morph, which lies somewhere between ahmar and adham (it is not clear where the perception of 'green' originates). 'Sinjari' is the highly prized, rare, dark morph Altai Saker (the Altai Falcon was the favourite of Atila the Hun). The Altai Falcon is thought to be a large subspecies originating from the Altai Mountain region in Central Asia. These sakers are never common, but rumour has it that the falcon dealers of Kabul, Afghanistan sell them.

The rare 'sinjari' saker is a large charcoal-grey colour and most commonly represents the 'Altai' subspecies.

Any female Saker Falcon is called 'hurr' by Arab falconers. Hurr is a word meaning noble or free and carries a strong connotation of masculinity. Again, because there has been little to no opportunity to observe breeding falcons, the Arabs have always assumed that a hurr is a male Saker Falcon. Conversely, the actual male Saker Falcon is assumed to be female, because of his inferior size, and has therefore been given the feminine name, 'garmoosha'. For those that have not had the opportunity to witness the actual side-by-side disparity in size between male and female falcons, it is hard to appreciate, aside from a similarity of plumage and body proportions, that the two actually belong to the same species. When questioned about their classification methods, many Arab falconers assert that the females of the 'hurr species' are the smaller ones, and the males are naturally the largest. The same applies to the 'garmoosha species', and incidentally to both sexes of the peregrine species. However, thanks to the recent advent of captive falcon breeding, things are finally getting sorted out, and the true facts are reluctantly being acknowledged. But as far as the vocabulary of a bird's gender is concerned, Arabs will continue to name them as they have done in previous generations.

The attributes that make the Saker Falcon the favoured bird in Arab falconry are many. Falcons generally exhibit two types of hunting techniques — the high speed stoop, and the chase and grab. As a desert falcon the Saker has adopted a relatively low-flying, 'search and chase' method of pursuit, which enables her to catch mammals as well as birds. Though slower in flight than a Peregrine, the Saker is in her element when chasing Houbara. The large body size and relatively large, buoyant wings give the Saker the stamina that is needed for desert hawking. This robust, 'rough and tumble' falcon is a 'gutsy' hunter that is not easily intimidated. She will readily engage in a fight on the ground with quarry twice her size, and her soft feathers, by comparison to the Peregrine, are less likely to be damaged in the resulting struggle that ensues once a Houbara has been caught. The Saker has long legs but lacks the extended, bird-catching toes of the Peregrine. Nevertheless, the relatively short, thick toes are powerful by comparison and aid in holding large quarry.

A striking feature that sets the Saker apart from most other falcons is her relatively large 'fluid' eyes. Although the number of rods and cones in the retina is not dissimilar to other falcons, some Arab falconers believe the Saker possesses superior eyesight and can accordingly spot Houbara at a greater distance.

The temperament of the Saker suggests that she may indeed be more intelligent than the Peregrine. What the Saker lacks in speed, she more than makes up for in tactical hunting skills. A series of feints, false attacks, deceitful manoeuvres and short cuts are often employed by this desert specialist. The Saker can be a difficult bird to tame, and her initial unwillingness to accept captivity is testimony to her intelligence. Eventually her wildness and difficult temperament give way to a resolute denial of food, and in the end her tameness and manageability is second to none. The ability to come through the tough, militant training necessary to bring her into line must further endear her to Arab falconers.

The Peregrine Falcon runs a close second to the Saker in overall popularity and is preferred by some Arab falconers. For the same reasons that apply to Sakers, mistakes have been made in regard to the sex and classification of the Peregrine. The popular, large female Peregrine is called 'shaheen' by Arab falconers, and the male is called 'tibba'. However, shaheen is masculine and tibba is feminine, or so it has been assumed. And until recently, similar to the Sakers, separate 'shaheen' and 'tibba' species were thought to exist — each made up of slightly larger males and slightly smaller females.

The Peregrine is faster and far more aerial than the Saker, and initially will lend itself much more readily to training. The above are paramount reasons that have helped establish the Peregrine as the falcon ideal for traditional falconry. But however utilitarian the Peregrine may be, in a desert environment against Houbara, she has a few shortcomings. She is 'stiff-feathered' and cannot endure the rigours of a ground tussle without risking damage to her flight feathers. Being a bird-catching specialist, she is far less willing to grab anything that is not in flight. All this can be a distinct disadvantage against Peregrine, since a defence tactic the Houbara may use is to land, extend its wings and puff up its feathers (so as to

This rough and tumble 'Ashgar Hurr' will readily tackle quarry twice its size in a ground tussle.

This Kairowan has just been caught by a "tibba" (male Peregrine Falcon) in immature plumage.

appear twice as large) and squarely 'challenge' an oncoming falcon. This method of intimidation can completely foil an inexperienced Peregrine. Furthermore, Peregrines do not withstand the disciplinary measures that are often required of a Saker, and when subjected to long periods of fasting the Peregrine is far more prone to stress-related illness. Additionally, Peregrines are notoriously slow moulters and most Arab falconers are reluctant to risk unnecessary damage to delicate, growing feathers. Therefore, the Peregrine is a poor choice as a 'starter' for the next falconry season. In fact, many Peregrines do not complete their moults before the end of the following season.

The Lanners, Luggers, Barbary Falcons and Red-naped Shaheens are either too small, too slight of build or too slow to be of much use in catching or handling Houbara and, therefore, are not highly valued. Consequently, the above four have been conveniently lumped into the lowly 'wichery' category, and little effort has been made to distinguish between them. The term, 'wichery shaheen', however, is often heard, and this undoubtedly applies to the Barbary Falcon or Red-naped Shaheen since these are strong, Peregrine look-alikes. It logically follows that the term, 'wichery hurr', must apply to the Lanner or Luggar. Wicheries have generally been relegated to the role of 'children's birds' or 'barak hawks' (see 'Capture of falcons'). However, new interest has been generated in the wichery shaheen females as they have proven their worth as 'Kairowan falcons'.

Capture of falcons

From September through to November millions of birds, and the raptors that feed on them, migrate across Arabia from Eastern Europe and Central Asia enroute to their southerly wintering areas (see chapter 5). With the shorter northern days and chill in the air that signals the onset of migration, each cold snap sends a new wave of raptors off on their great annual journey. Among this sea of bird life will be thousands of Saker and Peregrine Falcons. And waiting for their arrival over the regions of Syria, Iran, Pakistan and the Arabian Gulf will be the 'falcon trappers'.

All trapping methods involve luring falcons to the falconer with the pretence of the falcon finding an easy meal — and the pigeon is the classic bait used for this purpose. Falcons consider pigeons to be the ultimate delicacy, and most falcons, regardless of their species or size, will not hesitate to take one when the opportunity presents itself. Occasionally the suspicious nature of the 'wily' Saker Falcon will cause her to ignore a bait pigeon, and for those a gerbil is held in reserve, as this bait is irresistible to a Saker!

The actual methods used to capture falcons have changed little over the centuries. A lightweight frame, is fitted to the back of a bait bird and tied under the breast, in front of and behind the wings so as to permit flight. This 'shabichet hehmama' (noose harness), is covered with a dozen or more standing open-loop nooses, made from stiff nylon fishing line. In earlier days before nylon was available, the nooses were fashioned from woven strands of coarse horse or camel hair. A long line with a small weight at its free end may be attached

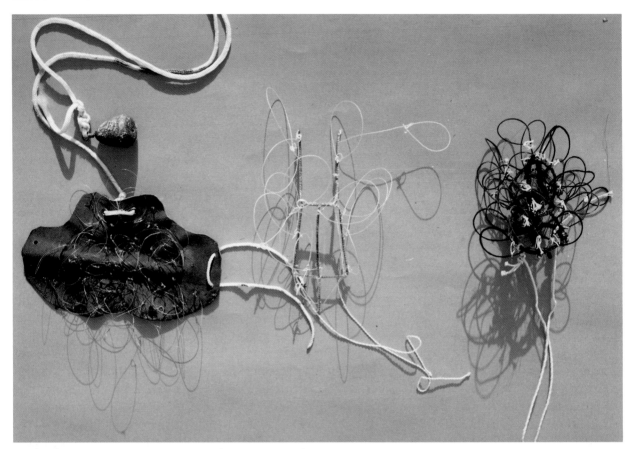

A western pigeon harness (right), a typical shabichet behmama (centre) and a nigil made from course camel hair (left).

to the frame to assist in retrieving the pigeon and the frame. Once released the slightly hampered flight of the bait bird signals injury or weakness to the falcon, and she is attracted to an easy meal.

Today the bait bird, with its noose frame attached, is thrown from a moving vehicle when a falcon is spotted. Care is usually taken to throw the pigeon from the side opposite the falcon. The object of this is to conceal any association of the pigeon with the trapper — the falcon ideally should think the pigeon has been struck by the vehicle. The falcon, if all goes as planned, will alight on top of the pigeon and, during the process of killing and eating it, will ensnare her long toes in one or more of the nooses. Although she can fly short distances with the pigeon attached to her feet, she cannot maintain this for long and eventually must land and confront her pursuers. She is caught!

Another method worth mentioning is one that utilises a falcon of 'little worth' to catch a more valuable one. Falcons will not hesitate to intimidate and rob a weaker, slower falcon of its catch if the opportunity presents itself — rivalry is strong among siblings, and it is vicious between species. A small falcon, such as a Luggar, is retained for this purpose. A single thread is passed through each lower eyelid (a painless process known as 'sealing' — see 'Training') and the lids are drawn up only

enough to prevent the falcon from seeing the ground when it flies. A lightweight frame, about the size of a hen's egg, is stuffed with feathers or fur to act as a bait decoy. Attached to the frame are many nooses. The 'nigil' (feather-noose bundle), is attached to the leg of a 'bizzuar' (lesser falcon). In the West the bizzuar is referred to as a 'barak hawk'. When a desirable falcon is sighted, the bizzuar is thrown into the air. Since its downward vision is impaired, it cannot see to land, and it flies upward, often in an awkward manner, carrying its decoy. To another falcon the opportunity to rob a lesser one proves irresistible. In this instance it is not the lesser falcon that is attacked but rather the decoy it carries. When the larger falcon becomes ensnared, continued flight for either is impossible, and both flutter to the ground uninjured.

A well-known Indian method for catching a falcon utilises a 1.5 metres high by 2-metre wide, fine wide-mesh net known as a 'dhogazza'. (The Arab equivalent is a 'shabichet hua'.) The net is loosely supported by two small poles. A gerbil or bait bird is tied to a peg in the ground approximately half a metre or so in front of the net.

Trappers insist that it is important to position the bait upwind of the falcon, as she will always fly into the wind to get it. For this reason the net is often slanted, 'lean-to' fashion, in the direction of the oncoming falcon. The slightest movement of the falcon's wings or body upon engaging the net will pull it off the poles and over the falcon. There is little chance for the falcon to get free of the net, for the more she struggles, the more entangled she becomes. By the time the trappers arrive on the scene, the falcon is usually tightly wrapped up in the net.

Although falcons have ultra keen eyesight it is not certain why they fly into the dhogazza. Two explanations suggest that they either mistake the fine netting for filaments of grass, or being intent on the bait, they dismiss the hazard until it is too late.

Another ingenious method of trapping a falcon, that has been likened to 'fishing the sky', involves the use of a 'kuhah' (a blind used by the trapper to hide behind), a 'shabichet jelb' (a net brought over the falcon by means of hinged supports) and a lure pole. The method works as follows — a 15-metre closed circuit line runs from the kuhah to a pole (of several metres height), then continues through an eyelet at the top of the pole, and angles down to another eyelet pegged into the ground approximately 10 metres from the pole, contuining back to the blind to complete the full circuit. The pegged eyelet on the ground is positioned to be in the exact centre of a concealed 'bow', hinged at both ends, to which a net has been attached. Exactly midway between the eyelet at the top of the pole and the one on the ground a pigeon fitted with a harness, is fastened to the line. When the line is relaxed, the pigeon rests on the ground. Pulling on one end of the line draws the pigeon into the centre of the bow-net, pulling on the other line draws the pigeon up the pole. By manipulating the lines the pigeon can be made to flip and flutter in a seemingly helpless manner. This action will attract the attention of raptors for kilometres in all directions. With luck, the trapper will soon be alerted to the presence of a falcon by the familiar 'hiss of air' rushing through her wings as she rockets out of the sky for a closer look. When she kills the pigeon and begins to pluck it, the trapper slowly draws in the pigeon, with the falcon in tow, into the centre of the shabichet jelb. A third line runs from the shabichet jelb directly to the kuhah. When this third line is pulled the net is brought over the falcon, and she is caught.

The most intriguing method of catching a falcon

The dhogazza is a fine wide-mesh net. The falcon becomes entangled as all its attention is focused on the bait.

is the 'hide', or 'dig in' approach. This method is known worldwide by falconers, and it is used by the American Indians to obtain eagle feathers for their traditional ceremonies. A stationary falcon is sighted a good distance away. A hole is quickly dug in the sand, and a trapper is buried except for his head and gloved hand(s). A basket (or some such item) is camouflaged with grass and placed over the man's head. The trapper can see out, but nothing can see into the basket. A pigeon is tied to a line which in turn is tied to the trapper's wrist. He then repeatedly tosses the pigeon in the air to attract the attention of the falcon. When the falcon kills the pigeon and begins to eat, the only thing out of the ordinary she sees is a glove sticking out of the sand. This poses no alarm to her. The glove slowly 'reels in' the unsuspecting falcon and pigeon, until, when she is within reach, the glove grasps the legs of the falcon, and she is caught!

Once a falcon is caught, by whatever method, a head-cloth is quickly thrown over the frantic and frustrated bird to prevent injury to herself and the trappers. She can then safely be grasped by her feet. A hood is then placed over her head. Finally, she is wrapped in an 'abba' (a type of straight-jacket formed from a square piece of cloth with the two corners of one side brought together and sewn down a central seam) to prevent her from extending her wings and damaging her feathers. The pockets formed house the falcon's shoulders, while the remainder of the cloth is wrapped around her feet and tail and tied with a strap. Thus 'packaged' she can be comfortably and safely transported in a prone position 'lying stomach down'.

Furniture

The equipment that is necessary for the restraint, housing, training and daily maintenance of a falcon is collectively referred to as 'the furniture'. Obviously, there must be a means of restraining a raptor, in a way that is non-objectionable, simply to prevent it from flying off when not being exercised or hunted. The ideal means of restraint involves a strong, but lightweight tether fitted to each ankle. These tethers or jesses, are referred to as 'subuq', and they are usually made of leather. Subuq are made of an extremely strong, resilient braided cord containing a high percentage of nylon, which has proven superior to leather for enduring the desert climate. The free ends of the subuq are then brought together and tied to a single, short, but thicker cord 10 to 20 centimetres in length. This piece is then fastened to a brass or steel swivel, which in turn is attached to another cord about a metre in length. This train comprises of a 'mursil' (leash components) and a 'midwar' (a swivel).

The subuq attached to the falcon's legs are connected to the mursil (2 leash pieces) and separated by a midwar (swivel). The wakir is a portable perch. Falcons are carried on a mangalah in the UAE and surrounding areas, and on a dass (gauntlet) in Qatar, Kuwait and some parts of Saudi Arabia. The burqa (hood) calms the falcon.

The perch upon which a falcon stands is called a 'wakir'. The wakir is often an ornate piece of furniture fashioned from a piece of durable hardwood which is turned on a lathe, varnished and upholstered. On one end there is a flat, disc-shaped perching surface, padded to minimise bruising of the falcon's feet, with a diameter of about 15 to 20 centimetres; just enough to permit the falcon to stand flat-footed on both feet. The other end is fitted with a steel spike that can conveniently be thrust into the ground. Immediately below the dish-like perching surface, the wooden body of the wakir narrows to a diameter sufficient to house the spike alone. There is a reason for this economy of size — it minimises weight. Traditionally the nomadic falconer, perched atop a camel had to carry not only the falcon but the bare necessities of her furniture. While the falcon was perched on the falconer's hand, she was also attached, by means of the mursil, to the wakir, which was in turn tucked under the falconer's arm.

The falconer requires a means of protecting his hand during the transportation of a falcon. While being carried a falcon stands and balances remarkably well. However, as this 'perch' is often moving it is necessary for the falcon to grip with its sharp and powerful talons. The traditional form of protection for a falconer's hand or arm is a leather glove or 'gauntlet', referred to by Arab falconers as a 'dass' or 'kaff'. The dass is used in and around the region of Qatar, and in some regions of Saudi Arabia. However, in the United Arab Emirates, Bahrain, Kuwait and most of Saudi Arabia, the dass has been replaced by a fabric-covered padded cuff, known as a 'mangalah'. The padding is often stiff camel hair or any excelsior-like material. The hand is slipped into one end of the mangalah, and the fingers grasp the subuq, or a short piece of mursil from the other end. As a security measure the end of the mursil can be fastened to the mangalah when it is not fastened to the wakir. Although many falconers find the mangalah awkward, it does offer practical value for the rougher aspects of desert hawking — firstly it allows the falcon to sink her talons into something substantial when the ride gets 'rough and bumpy', and secondly, a bare foot can be slipped into it as easily as a hand, and the falcon can be secured firmly against the floorboards of a vehicle bouncing across the dunes.

The 'burqa' (leather head cover or hood), that functions as a blindfold, is perhaps the single most indispensable piece of equipment known to the falconer. A raptor's world is mainly what it

An adult male Barbary Falcon standing on a wakir.

visualises; therefore, this burqa has the effect of psychologically removing the bird from any vision that would stimulate or upset it. The burqa assists in transforming a nervous, agitated, or otherwise emotionally upset raptor into a pseudo-hypnotic bird. A falcon that has been properly trained will accept a well-fitting, comfortable burqa and remain calm, without moving, for long periods of time (hours to days) seemingly oblivious to its noisy surroundings.

The burqa is fashioned from a pattern designed to comfortably and snugly fit over the falcon's head with only the beak protruding from an opening in the front. The hood is purposely distorted (enlarged) around the region of each eye, so as to ensure that the eyes do not touch the leather. Ideally, the fit should be such that no light enters any part of the hood when it is being worn by the falcon. The back of the hood is shaped so that the opening around the base of the falcon's skull can be slightly constricted, not too tight or uncomfortable, but enough to ensure that it cannot be removed by the falcon. The neck openings are 'closed' (narrowed) and 'opened' (widened) by means of leather 'drawstrings'.

23

An Arab falconer with a fine ashgar Saker Falcon during an afternoon training session.

There are several different hood styles. The typical Arab burqa is lightweight, and is fashioned from a one-piece pattern that, when sewn, holds its shape well despite being stuffed into pockets! An 'accordion pleating' arrangement in the back of the burqa is used to achieve closure. The 'Dutch' hood is generally an ornate, moulded work of art, and is formed from stretching the sewn and then soaked leather components over a specific mould (shaped in the form of a falcon's head). When the hood is dry, it is trimmed and later removed from the mould. An 'inverted V' is cut from the back, so that when the V is closed, the hood is drawn together to be a custom fit of the head. An 'Indian' hood is the simplest of the three. It is fashioned from a unique, one-piece pattern and, like the burqa it is not formed on a mould. It closes by means of a 'V' cut from the back.

All hood styles (Arab, Dutch, Indian or other) display some form of ornamentation on the top. Aside from the decorative aspect, the object functions as a convenient means of grasping the hood with the fingers of the right hand. This is essential in the process of placing the hood on the falcon's head (discussed under 'Training').

The object which is used to exercise the falcon during training, or to retrieve the falcon after an unsuccessful flight is called the 'tilwah'. (In western terminology it is referred to as the 'lure'.) The typical Arab tilwah is made, appropriately enough, of the wings of dead Houbara. The wings are tied together to form an attractive bundle. The device, when swung by a long cord, instantly attracts the attention of a falcon over great distances, and can be used to recall an errant falcon or simply exercise and condition a falcon for the rigours of the hunt.

When not in use, the tilwah must be hidden. This is achieved through a useful piece of furniture known as the 'miklah'. The miklah is a simple, white, canvas bag in which the tilwah and a few other items, such as a knife, are stored until needed. In contrast to the miklah, its western counterpart, the lurebag, is a highly ornate, many chambered, leather purse that is worn over the falconer's shoulder. There are pockets for the lure, one or more pigeons (used for training purposes), a leash, a whistle, one or more hoods and any other items that may be useful in the field. The lurebag is worn by the falconer in the field, while the miklah is stored in the hawking party vehicle until needed.

A proper hood must (1) be comfortable, (2) not make contact with the eyes, cere or lips, (3) the beak opening should be large enough to permit the falcon to eat though yet be snug enough to prevent the entry of any external light.

Training

It is a tall order to train wild falcons to chase, grab and grapple with quarry that is often twice their size. To do this upon command, at any given time of the day, and often in the intense heat of the desert sun requires the use of harsh and demanding methods. The primary aim of Arab falcon training is the rapid instillation of tameness and obedience without compensating courage.

Consider the following facts. Falcons and quarry arrive in the Arabian Gulf region at about the same time. There can be no time wasted in training, or the falconer risks losing much or all of the Houbara season, and the effort expended in training a falcon will have been for nothing. And the Arab falconer being under pressure to make the most of the situation at hand traditionally has not had the luxury of several months to train a new falcon while utilising an older, experienced one from the season before. Until recently, with the availability of luxuries such as air conditioning and suitable year-round food supplies, it was impractical to attempt to retain a falcon from one season to the next. The Arabian 'hot season' lasts from April to October. Being temperate climate birds, Sakers and Peregrines suffer in the unprotected heat of midsummer. Also, it was impractical for the nomadic falconer to keep falcons year-round as they had to be fed, and suitable food was not available during the hot, off-season. Therefore, most falcons, with the exception of star performers, were released at the end of a hunting season. Consequently, to reap the most from the desert, quick, direct and practical falconry training methods evolved.

When a falcon first comes into the hands of a trainer its eyes are usually 'sealed'. Specifically, a threaded sewing needle is passed through each lower eyelid at the centre of the thickened, feathered margin. The free ends of the thread are then pulled up to draw the eyelids up over the eyes (in birds only the lower eyelids are movable), and the ends are tied over the top of the bird's head. The procedure is painless, except for an initial

A Peregrine Falcon with a Houbara.

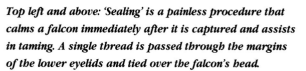

Top left and above: 'Sealing' is a painless procedure that calms a falcon immediately after it is captured and assists in taming. A single thread is passed through the margins of the lower eyelids and tied over the falcon's head.

prick, and the advantages it presents for taming are enormous. Birds in general are intensely visual creatures, and the majority of stimuli that governs their behaviour is perceived through their eyes. Blindfolding a freshly trapped falcon to the terrifying, new surroundings that confront her has a remarkable, almost hypnotic calming effect. Furthermore, the process of sealing permits a gradual restoration of sight and therefore a gradual, progressive introduction to the falcon's new visual world. When the lower lids are sewn up, they begin to sag on each side of the single thread after a few days. The sagging permits the gradual entry of light, which allows the falcon to begin to visualise faint images in her peripheral vision. It is during the sealed period that major progress in taming can be achieved, as the falcon comes to accept all the sounds and tactile sensations of her captive new world. Only when the sagging is pronounced and a little of the pupil becomes exposed can the bird focus on images. When this stage occurs the thread is removed, thus restoring full sight. The sealing period may last less than a week, but the falcon is most likely to emerge from this short experience in a totally tame, yet unstressed state of mind.

How does a falcon that has temporarily been deprived of her sight know to eat? First of all, it is not that important that the falcon eat during her first day or so in captivity. A certain amount of time is usually allowed to elapse before introducing the falcon to her first meal so as to take the edge off her initial wildness. When she begins to lose her defiance, the falconer will alert her to the presence of food by stroking her toes with something edible. This action presents more of an annoyance initially, and she will bite at the offending item. It is the job of the falconer to make sure she gets a good taste. At first she may only bite, but eventually when she resigns to her new surroundings, she will eat readily each time food is felt beneath her feet.

An initial reduction in weight is necessary to take the edge off her wildness and bring her into a receptive frame of mind for training.

The ideal weight to be maintained by a wild caught falcon in captivity, should be just low enough to keep her in a tame, manageable state of mind, and hungry enough to pursue quarry with keen intensity — but never low enough to jeopardise her health. A 10% reduction in a falcon's 'trapped' body weight is safe, and will generally suffice. Western falconers routinely record a falcon's weight when it is first caught, as a reference point for future conditioning. Most Arab falconers have not traditionally had access to scales to weigh their falcons. Keenness and condition have been determined by subjective and relatively insensitive methods — the 'attitude' of the falcon was judged, and the prominence of the 'keel' (ie. the lack of fat and muscle on each side of the carina of the breast bone) was felt. Obviously there is much room for error. Any Arab falconer that is consistently able to maintain his birds in a state of constant readiness and health using these antiquated methods, deserves to be recognised as a master. Fortunately, the more progressive Arab falconers now routinely use scales.

The necessity to temporarily blindfold or hood a falcon on an 'as needed' basis, to enhance her manageability under certain conditions, carries over throughout most of her daily life in captivity. For example, if one falcon is to be fed and others in the same room are not, it is best to hood the other falcons to prevent them from robbing or attacking the falcon that is eating. For this reason a falcon must be trained to accept the hood or burqa. No amount of writing can adequately describe the process of hooding a falcon; it can only be learned through experience and mastered by those with a delicate touch. If a falcon is sealed when she first

Adult Peregrine with a Houbara.

A Kuwaiti falconer and his bird. There is a unique rapport between man and bird.

comes into the hands of a falconer, she can be trained to accept the hood far more easily than if she were not. Hooding a sealed falcon is relatively easy, as the bird has no means of dodging and fighting what she cannot see coming. The gentle, repeated action of placing and removing the hood from the falcon's head soon causes her to accept it without the slightest objection.

The process of hooding requires that the job be done with the fingers of the right hand and the falconer's teeth, since the left hand is occupied with holding the falcon. The hood is usually held between the index and second fingers of the left hand and by the decorative plume, with the beak hole facing the thumb. The leather 'chinstrap', just below the beak opening, is brought up to where it just engages the lower mandible, and with the beak now protruding through the hole, the hood is simply 'rolled' over the head. The hood can then be tightened by means of the drawstrings or braces at the rear of the neck opening. One brace is again grasped between the fingers and the other between the teeth. A gentle, even pull in opposite directions tightens, or closes, the hood. To open it, for

removal from the falcon's head, the adjacent braces are pulled. It is interesting, from a westerner's point of view, that Arab trained falcons seldom, if ever, require the burqa be tightened. A falcon trained by a master Arab falconer is generally so well tamed ('manned') and 'made to the hood' that it will sit for hours with this loose-fitting object on its head without making any attempt to remove it.

The process of taming a falcon is known as 'manning'. It begins from the moment the bird first comes into the falconer's hands. The manning process is not a battle of wits or a contest of who can outlast who. Rather it is a progressive series of introductions from one new and potentially alarming scenario to the next, with positive reinforcement (food) being the reward for acceptance, and denial of food for obstinance. A falcon as a rule tames relatively easily (compared, for example to an accipitrine hawk), and most will rapidly progress through the process. The key to success is gentle persistence. A sealed falcon is progressively made to encounter as many sounds and tactile sensations as possible until her sight is fully restored. She is introduced to the sounds of crowds, men talking, laughing, shouting, children playing, dogs barking, automobile engines racing, horns, sirens, ie. anything that she would commonly encounter in captivity. She is carried on the mangalah, stroked on the breast, hooded and unhooded, etc. until she comes to accept the human touch without alarm or objection. If the falcon is not sealed the hood serves to remove the falcon from alarming visual stimuli.

To gradually introduce the falcon to her new environment, the hood is periodically removed for short periods of time. If the falcon should become overly alarmed the hood is promptly replaced. Patience must be exercised, and care must be taken that the manning process is not pushed too fast. Too much too soon can make a wild falcon hysterical, and what has taken days to accomplish can be undone in a careless minute! Each new confrontation is alarming and stressful to a falcon, and her reaction will be one of wildness and fear, followed by fatigue. The initial wildness and fear are tempered by hunger. Just enough reward is given when the situation is accepted and to carry the falcon over to the next training experience. As fatigue accumulates more and more introductions can be made until the bird comes to accept her new environment in total.

It is noteworthy that Arab falconer's birds are taught to respond to their names. All falconers worldwide name their birds, but this is for sentimental reasons and usually has no practical purpose. When Arab falcons are being fed, their trainers will often shout their names, so as to create a Pavlovian response. Many people have witnessed a hooded falcon standing calmly on its wakir suddenly bolt off in the direction of its shouted name.

When the falcon is sufficiently manned, she is introduced to the tilwah. The falcon's initial reaction to this foreign object is one of either alarm or apathy; therefore, to make it attractive it is garnished with meat, and the falcon is permitted to eat from it. She quickly comes to associate its appearance with food. After a few meals on the tilwah a 'conditioning' is established, and further garnishment is no longer needed. Thereafter, each time the falcon comes to the tilwah she is coaxed to release her grip on it and step onto the mangalah where she is rewarded with food, and the tilwah is placed back in the miklah.

The Houbara wing tilwah, when swung on its cord, is thought to simulate a flying Houbara as perceived by a falcon in the wild. Whether it actually does is doubtful, as a falcon can be trained to come to any object as long as she is fed from it. The purpose of the tilwah is simply to get the falcon's attention and bring her back to the trainer.

In the West an inexperienced eyass falcon can be exercised and educated by a method known as 'stooping to the lure'. The falcon is released and shown the lure. When she flies in to grab the lure, it is quickly jerked away before she makes contact with it. The falcon's momentum carries her past the expected point of impact, so that she must make a turn and try for a second pass. This can be repeated over and over again. The method conditions and rewards the falcon's persistence. A

The 'tilwah' (Arab-style lure) consists of Houbara wings tied together at the end of a cord, and is used as a training and retrieving device.

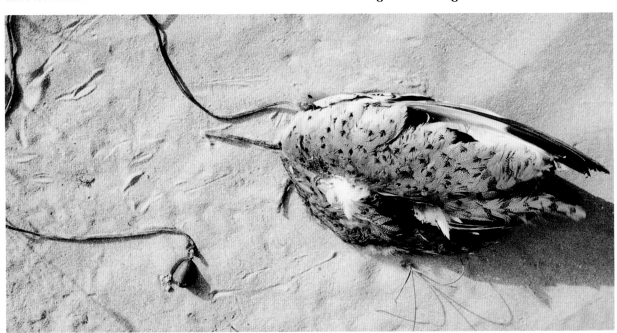

A well-known retainer of the late Sheikh Rashid bin Saeed Al Maktoum training his falcon. Photo, c. 1950 by Ronald Codrai.

A bedouin falconer in the sand retrieving captured quarry from his falcon.

novice falcon can be made to realise the advantage of height — the higher she goes, the faster she comes down, and the faster she comes down, the closer she comes to the lure. All of this has great advantage in teaching a falcon to fly high overhead in anticipation of quarry being 'flushed' directly under her (known as 'waiting on' in western terminology).

In the early stages of Arab training a falcon is exercised daily (sometimes twice daily) by means of the tilwah, but the exercise of stooping to the lure is generally not done. The Arab falconer, instead, sees a far greater advantage to repeatedly calling his falcon over a long distance. One man holds the hooded falcon, while a second man with the tilwah, who is positioned up to a half kilometre away, gives the signal to unhood and release the falcon. Most Arabs believe that this direct method of 'luring' best prepares a falcon for the conditions she will encounter in the desert — and they are absolutely right. To catch a Houbara a 'ringing-type-flight' is essential. This occurs when a falcon is released after quarry that is slightly slower in flight,

yet far more manoeuvrable in its evasive tactics. These flights are so named because they tend to 'ring' higher and higher until either the quarry is caught or the pursuing falcon becomes exhausted and quits the chase. The Houbara, with its massive wings, easily climbs to escape the falcon. Nevertheless, the well-muscled falcon is equal to the climb and eventually will close the gap and attempt to grab the Houbara. At that instant the Houbara usually makes a 90° turn (or greater), and the less manoeuvrable falcon must regain its composure, slowly turn, climb and again try to close the greatly increased distance created by the Houbara. In the end only a strong, persistent falcon will be rewarded.

We must assume that ringing flights for Houbara and Kairowan have evolved in Arab falconry because they are the practical flights that work for these quarry. A Houbara hawking scenario, in the open desert, does not favour a 'waiting on' situation, and consequently it is not used by Arab falconers. By the time a Houbara is located, usually at some distance, it is almost immediately off and flying, and there is no time to 'position' the falcon. But far more importantly, there is no advantage in having the falcon high over a Houbara. A falcon's manoeuvrability is sacrificed by its stooping (diving) speed. The 'falling missile' would almost inevitably be dodged by the highly manoeuvrable Houbara, and the momentum of the falcon's stoop would place her well out of position and at a great disadvantage for catching up again.

A Houbara Bustard, generally being twice the size of a pursuing falcon, is not a natural prey species for the Saker or Peregrine. For this reason, these falcons, regardless of how hungry they can be made to be, are reluctant to take on such formidable quarry without a proper step-by-step introduction to alleviate their fears.

Enter the 'jessir'. Jessir is the Arabic word for any captive quarry that is to be used for entering (introducing or familiarising) a falcon to the quarry. A falcon is first allowed to eat from a freshly killed Houbara. A certain amount of fear is lost when the falcon, feeling the large but unthreatening bird under her feet, plucks the Houbara's feathers and eats her fill of the delectable meat. Next, a Houbara that is handicapped in such a way that it cannot fly to its fullest capability may be offered. If the falconer gives this bird to the falcon with his hands, the falcon will feel a certain degree of reassurance — that it is 'safe' — and will come to it. When the falcon approaches, the falconer may choose to release the Houbara and leave the falcon on her own with the jessir. If the falcon takes the Houbara, so much the better. If she refuses, a little food is withheld from the falcon, and the jessir is recaptured for the next day's lesson. If the falcon captures the jessir the falconer rushes in and quickly rescues the Houbara by substituting it with a freshly killed pigeon (equally delectable to the falcon). The Houbara can then be used again or released. At this point the falcon is considered 'entered to the quarry', and training is complete.

Before dismissing the subject of training altogether, the topic of hunger conditioning warrants discussion. It plays an important role in training as it brings the falcon into a receptive frame of mind for her education, and is regarded as the single most important factor in determining whether a falcon will be successful in a chase. However, it is important to understand that much conditioning of falcons is established by the mere creation of a training and feeding 'schedule'. For example, a falcon initially may only progress from one difficult stage of her training to the next through the feeling of sharp hunger. However, once a particular stage of training is achieved, thereafter, an associated task requires less hunger each time the task is to be achieved. Eventually the bird will

A falconer letting his falcon feed from a hare in the Empty Quarter.

come to relish the task, simply because it is part of her daily routine.

While a hunting party is in the desert, the sighting of a Houbara demands immediate action. Therefore, Arab-trained falcons need to be kept in constant readiness. If a falcon is not ready, the opportunity to catch the quarry is lost. But keeping a falcon in a state of readiness, to pursue something twice her size, at any time of the day, and often in the intense heat of the day, is a very tall order. To approach this level of readiness, extreme hunger must be generated. Obviously, razor-sharp readiness cannot be maintained for long — a day or two at most without sacrificing muscle mass, and subsequent strength and endurance — before risking a falcon's health seriously. All of this implies that conditioning a falcon, to meet the demands of the desert and the rigours of the Houbara hunt, relies upon a schedule which fluctuates between periods of extreme hunger (negative nitrogen balance) and periods of 'glut' and restoration (positive nitrogen balance). Without jeopardising its well-being, a falcon simply cannot be maintained at the fixed, relatively low body weight needed to produce 'hunger' over a prolonged period of time. The true master falcon intuitively knows when to provide his falcon with the necessary rest and restoration in preparation for the next period of readiness for the hunt.

Evolution of falconry in Arabia

Within the past decade modern western veterinary medical care for captive falcons of the Gulf region has become a recent and welcome development for falconers. Surprisingly, modern medicine has met with little resistance from the rigidly traditional bedu falconers. It appears that traditional remedies of 'branding', 'burning', 'smoking', 'salting' and the like have done little to generate confidence in their efficacy. Quite the opposite — it seems frustration with the ineffectiveness of the old ways has caused the 'new medicine' to be welcomed with open arms. The introduction of biotelemetry (which consists of an electronic transmitter/ monitoring device attached to a falcon) within the last few decades has revolutionised the world of falconry. Arabia is no exception. Before this technology was available, the loss of a hunting falcon during a chase was common. Indeed, the better the falcon was at what it was trained to do, the greater were the chances that it eventually would be lost. The qualities a falconer desires in his bird are that she be relentless in her desire to chase and that she possess the speed and endurance necessary to bring the drama to a successful conclusion. A strong falcon released after strong quarry provides excitement and spectacle, especially if the distance that initially separates the falcon and her quarry is great. But a great deal of anxiety is added to the excitement when the chase goes out of the sight of the falconer. In the days before telemetry, finding the falcon was often a matter of sheer luck, and finding the falcon before she had 'taken her fill' and gone to roost for the night, occasionally to be eaten by an owl, was Divine Providence! Telemetry has removed much of the anxiety of hunting with a falcon, as it has dramatically reduced the percentage of falcons lost.

Biotelemetry basically consists of three components — a transmitter, a 'directional' antenna and a receiver. The small transmitter weighing only a few grams is attached either to the falcon's leg or to a central tail feather by means of a permanently fixed clip. The location is the choice of the falconer. Transmitters are powered by two or three watch batteries and designed to emit continuous pulsating signals within the frequency of radio waves. The usual distance of an unobstructed 'line of sight' signal that can effectively be received ranges between 10 to 30 kilometres, depending on the quality of the transmitter. Breaks in the straight line of sight such as hills and valleys greatly reduce the range of transmission. The 'directional' antenna receives the strongest pulsating signal when held in the direction of the transmitter, and this message is given to the receiver. The receiver converts the message into an audible and visual form that can be monitored.

When a falcon disappears from sight, and it appears that she has no immediate intention of returning, the falconer strolls to the hawking vehicle and turns on the receiver. He scans the direction where the falcon was last seen with the

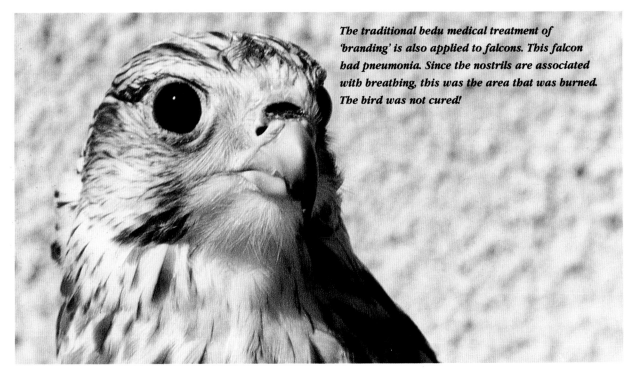

The traditional bedu medical treatment of 'branding' is also applied to falcons. This falcon had pneumonia. Since the nostrils are associated with breathing, this was the area that was burned. The bird was not cured!

A group of falcons on display in the souq. (Left to right): A Peregrine, two Sakers and two Lanners.

directional antenna. If the falconer has practised so as to be thoroughly familiar with the equipment, there will be no time lost in locating the bird.

Thirty years ago hawking was done from the back of a camel. The distance that could be covered in a day was usually limited to a few dozen kilometres. Therefore, the geographical scope of nomadic Arab hawking was limited to local tribal territories within the falconry regions of the Arabian Peninsula. Then the quarry, as would be expected, was far more abundant. Today, where Houbara still congregate in 'relative' abundance, deluxe, specially equipped airliners transport large hawking parties, with their falcons, to vast, designated 'Arab hawking areas' within Pakistan and Northern Africa. The camel has been replaced by custom made, open-topped, four wheel drive vehicles. Some vehicles have even been equipped with specially designed hydraulic seats that can be raised to heights of a metre or more so as to give the falconer greater visual scope over the terrain. Car phones communicate sightings of Houbara to other vehicles within the hunting party. As a result the hunting areas, some of which are the size of small countries, can be scoured with 'unerring' efficiency.

Changes were inevitable. The relatively recent discovery of oil in Arabia has opened the floodgates to unimaginable wealth and the modern technology and luxuries that follow it. This new wealth has left its mark on everything. Although falconry remains a major link to the nomadic past, it has not been totally immune to some minor alterations, especially when the alterations are presented in the form of convenience and luxury.

Although 'hawk souqs' have always been common place in the Middle East, many Arab falconers have preferred to rely more on their own trapping skills than their bargaining powers in the quest for falcons. It was simply more fun. Prior to the discovery of oil, fair and equitable prices for falcons were established according to a basis of supply and demand. However, today the price of an outstanding falcon is essentially whatever a wealthy sheikh will pay for it. Resultantly, prices for these market goods have become over inflated. More and more 'would be' hawk trappers and hawk merchants have been lured into this old profession, in the hope of making a quick fortune. As a result there may be more falcons to be found in the souqs today than ever before. Yet sadly, as one may well imagine, not all of the 'nouveau dealers' possess the expertise to keep their wares in fit and healthy condition. Therefore, the number of truly pristine falcons to be had at the beginning of a season is probably no greater today (and may even be less) than it was in the past.

THE HUNT

Just as the tradition of Arab falconry has been preserved and carried over to the present relatively unchanged, the rituals associated with the hunt itself have also been preserved. Today, although there is no longer a need for large groups of people to suddenly be displaced from their homes with little forewarning, the call of "Yallah!" (let's go!), still characterises the onset of the hunt.

Large hunting parties are headed by sheikhs, and the larger and more 'formal' the party is, the greater will be the effort to shield any information suggesting an exact departure date. The idea is to 'ready' the falconers so that they will have their bags packed, and their falcons ready at a moment's notice. Whether this 'necessary unexpectedness' is a carry-over from the need for sudden tribal movement, or simply an expansion of the philosophy that states, "Houbara have been found , they will not wait, you must be ready!", is speculative. Certainly the anticipation enhances the experience.

A typical hunting trip scenario would be as follows — a scouting party reports that large numbers of Houbara have been seen in the eastern desert region of Pakistan. That is where we will accompany the Sheikh on this particular visit. Word was, nine days ago, that we would leave 'tomorrow' at 10:30 a.m. The passports of all those attending the hunt are collected that night at the Sheikh's majlis. We had only to show up the next morning with luggage (packed with enough of the basics to last several weeks) and our falcons. Suddently the hunt is postponed for two days, and the departure time moved to 2:00 p.m. During the following three days the Sheikh is out of the country

An immature Peregrine Falcon and Houbara. After impact they spiralled to the ground in an entangled mass.

37

on business, so nothing is expected to happen. Upon his return, everyone waits for the 'call'. We hear nothing for a couple of days. People are beginning to wonder if the hunt is going to happen — rumours begin to circulate that the whole plan is to be tabled until next month. Then suddenly, we are told to be at the airport by 10:00 a.m. Yallah!

The flight on the air bus from the Gulf to Karachi would be the last travel luxury to be seen for many days to come. Once landed our gear is gathered, and we prepare to board another plane, only this time it is a Hercules C-130. The luxury is gone — we sit on duffel bags with our falcons, listen to the loud drone of the propeller-driven engines and watch frost form on the walls. The outside view from the cockpit shows patches of snow on the hills and lots of cloud-cover directly below. Occasionally, whenever the clouds breakup, the remnants of a mud and stone village can be seen. Eventually the plane touches down at a primitive landing strip in the desert. The only thing to be seen, in any direction — other than dust blowing from the hard pack of the runway — are eight open-topped, 4WD vehicles, and a rutted track.

Apart from the larger and rarer 'Altai-type' Sakers, the asbgar colour Saker is thought to be the most powerful and courageous; making it the classic bird of Arab falconry.

The gear is thrown into the vehicles. The falcons are braced against the wind with their talons firmly wrenched into their respective mangalahs. We are off again. After approximately one hundred kilometres we enter a dry river bed. The surrounding landscape divides into rocky outcrops and sand dunes, and when the sun sets it turns cold.

Although the rutted path along the river bed is periodically lost in the dim headlights, the relentless speed of the vehicle has not slackened. Finally, off in the distance the lights of the camp can be seen.

This modern Arab hunting camp, in contrast to the trip out to the camp, is anything but rough. The conveniences of modern living have taken the rough edges off the traditional camp, but the basic framework still remains. The large hunting camp is cordoned off with desert brush, and divided into sections made up of tent complexes.

Each complex consists of two to four tents, with its own generator for electrical power, and a compliment of servants and cooks. Instant telephone communication is provided by satellite booster stations, and there is even a camp physician in attendance.

A working garage or 'motor pool', operates all night, if necessary, to attend to the daily maintenance of the vehicles.

A large group of falcons 'weathering' (in falconers' jargon) in the sun before a hunt.

Once the gear is unloaded and living spaces are established, it is time to freshen up and pay our respects to the Sheikh. The Sheikh's tent is located in the centre of the camp, and we gather around in the clearing outside it. The campfire is strewn with Arab coffee pots and the perimeter of the clearing surrounded by falcons staked out on their wakirs. Fenced with densely piled desert brush, the edge of the clearing acts as a windbreak, and offers privacy from adjacent tent compounds. As the flickering campfire silhouettes the falcons against the desert brush, hunt stories begin to unfold. Coffee is drunk until the Sheikh signals that it is time to call it a night.

There is no time lost getting to sleep this night. The weight of the heavy, deep-piled cotton and wool blankets is a pure luxury in the cold of the desert night. Unexpectedly, the early morning call to prayer sounds. In the darkness of the tent someone murmurs, "This must be a dream, it cannot be morning yet." There is the smell of wood smoke, but this is probably the coals smouldering from last night's fire. Then someone from outside the tent opens the flap, leans in and says, "Would you like *chai* (tea)?" The night was far too short.

Before getting the morning's instructions, there is just time for a very quick breakfast. Fresh batteries have been placed in the transmitters (see chapter two), and the 'bleeping frequency' of each transmitter is noted. The transmitter that has been handed to me bleeps only on channel 9. I must remember this.

The little transmitter with its trailing wire antenna is clipped onto the falcon's tail feather. The hooded falcon, wakir, miklah and a few pigeons are stowed, as comfortably as possible, between my legs and on the floor of the hawking vehicle. It is 7:35 a.m. and we are off, single-file, into the morning mist!

The country that we are heading for is gentle — consisting of smooth, rolling dunes peppered with Artemisia brush. The path to that country is a deep rutted, sandy track that threatens to bury the wheels every 10 metres. Engines rev at a strained pitch as we bump and lurch through the mire. Off in the distance is a flat gravel plain, and beyond that, about three kilometres away, a grassy area comes into view. When we reach the gravel we are off and running at a speed that causes most of the vehicles to become airborne each time a small swell in the ground is encountered. The grassy area is a bit of a bog in places, so we slow down.

Beyond this is the vast dune area, barely seen through the shimmering heat waves that obscure the horizon. Suddenly the lead car stops. Two Houbaras have just been 'bumped' from the grassy cover. This was unexpected. A falcon has been released after them, but this must be a fruitless endeavour; at least three quarters of a kilometre separates the falcon from the nearest Houbara. I am amazed the falcon would even consider the situation. Soon she breaks off the chase, sets her broad wings on 'glide mode' and begins to circle upward in the rising thermal currents. In the distance falconers are trying to get her attention with a series of shouts. Several tilwahs are frantically tossed in the air. This bird, seemingly oblivious to the happenings below, appears to be revelling in the luxury of the morning thermals. Finally a pigeon on a long line appears and the falcon folds up and gently sails down to the falconer. This particular falcon will not be tried again until later in the afternoon.

Now we have reached the vegetated dunes. The long train of vehicles breaks up into singles, and the only contact we have with the rest of the group is by car phone. We creep along over the dunes very slowly now. All eyes are on the ground in search of Houbara tracks. A set of tracks was spotted a while ago, but they were old; they were 'weathered' impressions that lacked the crispness we are looking for. But now a new set of meandering tracks is found. These are fresh! Someone comments, "This one was eating here this morning." A man gets out of the vehicle and gently strokes across the top of the track with a blade of grass. The early morning dew is gone, but these tracks still hold all the fresh detail from the evening's moisture. Single grains of sand can be sheared off the relatively sharp edges of the impressions.

A falcon is brought up from the floorboard of the vehicle. The falconer manages to free the tightly tied subuq from the mursil. The braces on the burqa are drawn open, but for now the burqa is left on the bird's head. The falcon on the mangalah is held high and ready as we creep along, following the tracks. The falcon is restless and turns around to face the wrong direction. The bird is quickly redirected and we continue to creep ahead. Suddenly, by surprise, the Houbara gets up some 75 metres from the vehicle and 90° to the port side!

The black and white 'flash' of the wing, as the Houbara lifts off, is unmistakable. Again, the falcon is facing the wrong way! She is whisked around and the burqa is removed. It takes only a second

for the falcon to regain her balance. Her stare is fixed. She bobs her head once and bolts off toward the Houbara. The Houbara is now well on the wing and rising. Though the brightness obscures our view, we can still see the relatively slow but powerful, deliberate wingbeats of the Houbara going straight off from the left of the vehicle, rising into the sun. Everyone fumbles to get their sunglasses on for a better view. The Houbara's distance had become nearly a hundred metres by the time the falcon was finally off, but suddenly that distance has been reduced to a mere 20 metres. Both birds are at full speed, but the falcon is slightly faster. Slowly the gap is closing. The falcon chops away at the air with sharp, rowing wing-beats, two for every one of the Houbaras. About one quarter of a kilometre away from us now, the falcon reaches to grab the Houbara. A quick flip of the Houbara's wing hurtles it in a direction 90° away from the sun, and suddenly there is a huge distance between it and the falcon again. At least this time the two can be seen clearly. Both are still rising. Again, but more slowly than before the gap begins to close, only this time the falcon appears to be gaining a height advantage. Binoculars are pulled from the glove compartment. Within half a minute (that seems more like ten) the falcon reaches to grab again. And again, the same manoeuvre separates the two. The falcon is showing signs of fatigue, and so is the Houbara — but the Houbara seems to have the edge. Again, some thirty metres separates them. The distance between the birds is closing at a much slower pace. Still the falcon presses on. The falcon no longer attempts to rise over the Houbara. Perhaps she cannot. Once more the falcon slowly closes the gap, but now she appears to be off to the side of the Houbara, as if she wants to pass it. Those with binoculars clearly can see this is exactly what is happening. The two are now rowing along abreast of each other, at an altitude of about 150 metres. The falcon appears to overtake the Houbara on the right side, then she suddenly and sharply anchors to the left just as the Houbara makes the same turn. The two come together in an awkward flurry of wings, and this entangled mass slowly spirals down towards the ground. Cheers go up from everyone. The engine is started and we blast off in the direction of this drama to reclaim the falcon and her reward. The falcon will be amply rewarded. The remains of the Houbara will be this evening's supper. The story of today's events will live on for discussion at another campfire.

This 'jernass' (adult plumage) Peregrine is an experienced, seasoned favourite of a sheikh.

GENERAL FEATURES OF BIRDS OF PREY

Birds of prey, or raptors as they are more simply known, have evolved into the ultimate flying machine. They make their living by catching and eating other animals (carrion eaters being the exception), which obligates them to be stronger, faster, and generally more intelligent than the animals they prey upon. Since some species of hawks and falcons subsist almost entirely on birds, their flying skills are at the apex of aerial specialisation. Our fascination with raptors, aside from their beauty and regal gestalt, most often stems from their phenomenal aerial capabilities.

Flight

Before it is possible to appreciate refined and specialised flight, it is important to examine the features that are necessary for flight in general. People have often tried to imagine what it would be like to glide effortlessly on currents of air. This imagining is a misconception, and is illustrated by man's comical first attempts at flight. The fastening of 'wings' to outstretched arms has never resulted in a successful flight.

Flight, without the aid of machines or gadgets, is work in the extreme, which can only be accomplished with a great deal of strength and a huge expenditure of energy. The strength and energy required would only be possible through profound alterations in the anatomy and physiology of ground bound animals.

The ability to fly requires that the body weight of the flier be supported on a foil of air pressing against outstretched wings. If we were to consider our outstretched arms as wings, the force required to support our body-weight would be the same as

Brahminy Kite in flight.

43

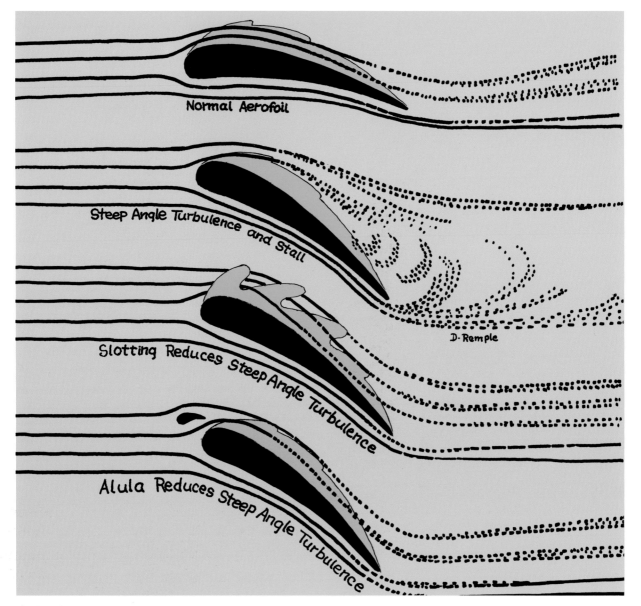

Normal Aerofoil

Steep Angle Turbulence and Stall

D. Remple

Slotting Reduces Steep Angle Turbulence

Alula Reduces Steep Angle Turbulence

The upper surface of a bird's wing is convex, the lower, concave. It is thickest at its leading edge like the wing or propeller of an aeroplane. As air moves over the wing, two forces are generated — a lift force acting on the bottom (created by air travelling faster over the upper surface), and a drag force opposing forward motion. When the wing angle is too great air-stream separates from the upper surface, causing turbulence, and the wing stalls. The drag force is greatest at the wing tips. The alula and feather slotting reduce drag.

that required of a gymnast performing the iron cross on the suspended rings (a feat that only a few professional athletes have developed the strength to accomplish). And this would only be the equivalent of 'gliding' or 'soaring'. Most birds need to create an aerofoil capable of supporting themselves when upward currents are not enough, and this requires forward motion. Therefore the ability to 'flap' the wings downward and backward is required. For man to accomplish this would be the equivalent of performing repeated 'iron cross' pushups!

All this only serves as an example of mankind's inability to do what birds do most commonly.

The strength birds use for flight is derived from a relatively huge pectoral muscle mass, and a vastly more efficient (relative to ourselves) oxygen delivery system to feed the muscles. The main muscles used to achieve flight are located on each side of the breast bone, which is a large thin, broad plate of bone designed to accommodate them. Were we able to fly, our pectoral muscles, in comparison to those of a bird, would minimally, have to be the size of two large pillows; one on each side of the mid-line — the combined weight of which would comprise approximately one-third of our body weight.

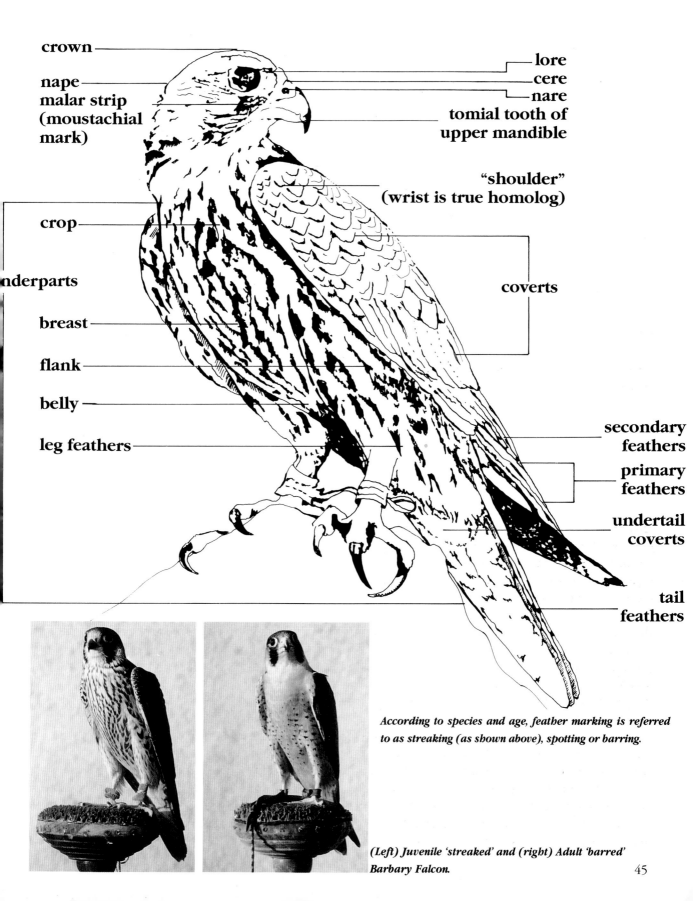

crown

lore
cere
nare

nape
malar strip
(moustachial
mark)

tomial tooth of
upper mandible

"shoulder"
(wrist is true homolog)

crop

coverts

nderparts

breast

flank

belly

leg feathers

secondary
feathers

primary
feathers

undertail
coverts

tail
feathers

*According to species and age, feather marking is referred
to as streaking (as shown above), spotting or barring.*

*(Left) Juvenile 'streaked' and (right) Adult 'barred'
Barbary Falcon.*

45

Without increasing bone weight, birds have developed large, strong skeletons to accommodate their huge muscle mass. The efficiency of the skeleton has been accomplished through an evolutionary fusion of numerous ancestral bones to form large, broad, pneumatic (air-filled) plates. The most striking example is the breastbone.

Respiratory System

Perhaps the most interesting feature that enables birds to fly, and here raptors excel, is their cardiovascular-respiratory (oxygen delivery) system. Though not intended as a book on avian physiology and anatomy, this system is worth mention, because it is nothing short of phenomenal, and serves as another prerequisite feature for flight that ground bound creatures lack.

Consider that the energy expended during flight is something we are incapable of summoning, even under rigourous athletic training. Also, consider that birds require and expend this kind of energy at altitudes where we would not be able to survive without supplemental oxygen.

A brief comparison of a bird's respiratory system with our own reveals their oxygen extracting superiority. During inspiration our lungs are inflated with air, and oxygen diffuses across the ultra thin barrier from the lung surface into the

The large breastbone is designed to accommodate the huge pectoral muscles for flight.

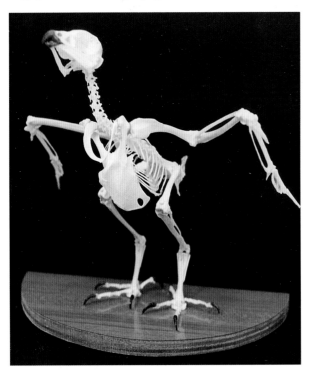

blood, and waste gases diffuse the other way to the exterior. Our lungs are 'dead end' sacs made up of millions upon millions of microscopic balloons known as alveoli.

Birds have no diaphragm and their lungs are not 'dead end' sacs. Birds breathe by means of large paired membranous air sacs, which draw air in through the lungs and blow air out through the lungs in a bellows-like fashion. These bellows (the air sacs) afford birds approximately four times the tidal volume of air that can be taken in with each breath, hence four times the oxygen. The action of the ribs moves air into and out of the air sacs. Additionally, during flight, the action of wings, not just the ribs, operates the bellows. The lungs of birds do not inflate and deflate as they do in mammals, but constantly absorb oxygen each time air moves through them. This alone makes them far more efficient than man.

This gives a brief glimpse at the remarkable system that enables flight. This system permits the American Golden Plover to fly over 3,000 kilometres non-stop between Alaska and Hawaii, and the Arctic Tern to migrate from Pole to Pole within a single year, a trip totalling 30,000 kilometres. Aircraft have collided with birds at altitudes over 11,000 metres. It is at a high altitude that the energetic superiority of birds becomes obvious — birds can perform work (flying) at altitudes where mammals would quickly perish at rest.

When we consider the physiological attributes necessary for flight, our appreciation for the superior athletic abilities of raptors is brought into perspective. Magnificent bird-catching raptors, such as the Peregrine Falcon or the lightning-quick little Sparrowhawk, have refined these skills to such an extent that they represent the epitome of aerial acrobats.

Eyesight

In general, birds are intensely visual creatures, and possess superior eyesight compared to most other animals. Raptors generally possess more superior eyesight than other birds. A simple indication is the size of the eyeball, or globe, in relation to the size of the head. A falcon's eyes occupy 15 times more space within their heads than those of humans. It is not the elephant but rather a bird that possesses the biggest eye of all terrestrial creatures — the eye of the African ostrich is five times the size of the human eye.

The Houbara Bustard, with its laterally directed eyes may turn its head to clearly focus with one eye on an object.

The forward directed eyes of the falcon gives it greater binocular vision.

Raptors, especially owls, tend to have more forward directed eyes than those of other birds. The eyes of prey species such as pigeons, are located within the sides of the cranium, which affords a greater visual field (a great advantage in avoiding predators). However, the location of the eyes of raptors affords them far greater binocular vision, since they are able to focus and coordinate the movement of each eye on the same object. Due to the relatively huge size of raptor's eyes, little space exists to accommodate eye movement and the muscles that produce it. With the exception of some small movement, bird's eyes are largely fixed within their skulls. To compensate for this drawback, birds have at least twice the number of cervical vertebrae as most mammals. This feature enables them to turn their heads upside down or to rotate their head on its axis almost 360 degrees.

Raptors have their own 'eye skeleton', which consists of a series of bony plates embedded within the tough outer layer, or tunic, of the eyeball. The plates offer support in maintaining the shape of the relatively large fluid-filled eye.

The mechanism of visual accommodation (focusing) is entirely different in mammals and birds. Here again, birds seem to have a clear superiority. Mammals focus by changing the shape of the lens, by means of a single muscle. Birds focus by means of two groups of individual muscles acting on the lens and the ability to distort the cornea by the action of a third muscle. Furthermore, a bird's lens is more elastic than that of mammals.

The retina of the eye is the highly complex, light-sensitive, nervous layer that transmits visual images via the optic nerve to the brain. The mammalian retina has only one region of acute vision — located in the area that receives the most light. Whereas the retina of birds — receiving light from every incoming angle — has all-round sharpness (visual acuity). The special light-sensitive cells within the retina are of two types — rods and cones. Rods are generally sensitive to the intensity of incoming light, whereas cones are sensitive to different wave-lengths within the colour spectrum. Colours are generally visualised in daylight but not at night. Night vision relies on the sensitivity of rods and not cones. Therefore, it stands to reason that nocturnal birds such as owls, possess relatively more rods than cones, and diurnal birds such as falcons, hawks, eagles and vultures, possess relatively more cones than rods.

Most creatures possess a third eyelid (nictitating membrane) which periodically flashes across the surface of the eye to lubricate the cornea. In raptors the nictitating membrane is largely transparent, and can serve the dual purpose of acting as 'goggles' during extremely fast flight.

Hearing

As mentioned above, birds are largely visual animals; therefore, hearing plays a secondary role in their survival. Vocalisation is complex and functions in every aspect of living from mating to defence. In general, a bird's hearing is equal to ours. Birds, however, have the ability to differentiate individual sounds much faster than humans. By recording the song of a Whip-poor-will, and playing it back eight times slower, it was discovered that the Whip-poor-will should be named the "Whip-pup-poor-will". Human ears are incapable of hearing the extra syllable. Furthermore, the recordings of a Mocking Bird that was imitating a Whip-poor-will were also played back eight times slower, and he too was singing, "whip-pup-poor-will"!

Among raptors, it is the nocturnal ones that have sharpened and refined their auditory senses. Although their night vision is tremendous by comparison to ours, they are additionally assisted by extraordinarily sensitive hearing, which helps them locate prey in the dark. Small, stiff feathers located around owls eyes make their eyes appear larger, but have no influence whatsoever on eyesight. They act as "parabola shields" for receiving sound. Furthermore, the owl's ear openings are situated at slightly different levels in the skull, so that with the aid of the feathered shields each ear receives sounds at slightly different times. This time delay of 0.00003 seconds confers a type of 'sound radar', which assists the owl in locating prey. Much like bats, owls can hone in on any sound-producing object, even in the total absence of visible light.

Feeding Adaptations

A universal characteristic of all birds of prey is the hooked beak, which is used for tearing and eating the flesh of their prey. Eating is accomplished by holding food down with the feet and tearing off bite-size pieces by an upward pull of the beak. Although the beak appears to be a formidable weapon in most raptors, only falcons possess well developed biting muscles and attempt to use the beak in self defence. The real weapons of most raptors, used for catching, killing prey and self defence, are their feet.

Swallowed food does not immediately enter the stomach of raptors; instead, it is temporarily stored in a sac-like dilatation of the esophagus known as the crop. Here it is softened, and undergoes some rudimentary digestive processing before it is allowed to enter, piece-by-piece, into the first of two stomachs for true digestion. The first is a pear-shaped glandular stomach — the proventriculus — similar to the mammalian stomach. Here glandular secretions for digestion are produced. Semi-digested food then passes into the 'muscular stomach', the ventriculus, where the semi-digested mass is 'chewed' or macerated and digestion is completed. The ventriculus in most birds is the familiar gizzard. A true gizzard is a powerful grinding organ containing stones (eaten by the birds), which assist in the maceration of the food. Raptors lack true gizzards, and possess weak muscular stomachs in comparison to other birds.

One peculiar feature displayed by all raptors is the formation of pellets (known as 'castings' in falconer's jargon), which are formed from indigestible material in the ventriculus and later regurgitated. Generally, the fur and feathers, and large bone pieces, especially in owls, remain undigested. This matter is ground and formed into a smooth egg-shaped pellet and regurgitated, usually before the next day's meal. Aside from ridding the stomach of indigestible material, pellet formation aids in the 'scrubbing' of the muscular stomach lining.

An interesting behavioural feature displayed by many diurnal and nocturnal raptors is 'food caching'. During seasons of plenty, when raptors are confined to their familiar hunting and breeding territories, and when food availability is at a premium, prey may be caught and stored in convenient hiding places for future use. The 'cache' provides a handy larder for the feeding of young during the breeding season.

Feathers and moulting

The unique and outstanding physical characteristic of birds is the possession of feathers. There are specialised types of feathers, each with separate functions. Broadly speaking, down feathers insulate the body against heat loss, contour feathers cover, streamline and insulate against environmental temperature extremes, and flight feathers provide the aerofoil necessary for flight. The flight feathers of many species display modifications which provide for specialised flight requirements. For example, the extremities of the major flight feathers at the tips of the wings of soaring raptors

Eagle Owl (left) and Barbary Falcon (right) 'castings'.

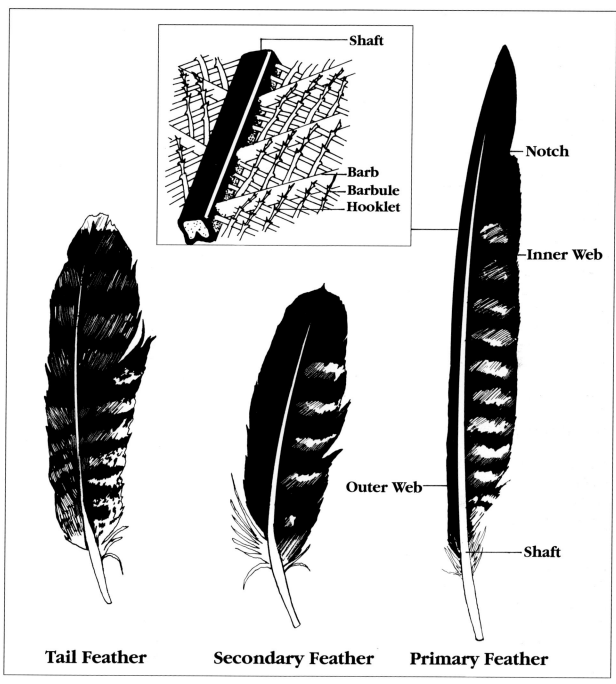

Shaft

Barb
Barbule
Hooklet

Notch

Inner Web

Outer Web

Shaft

Tail Feather　　　**Secondary Feather**　　　**Primary Feather**

like eagles, buzzards and vultures, abruptly narrows to form conspicuous notches, which, when the wing is spread, causes the feathers not to overlap each other but rather be separated by slots. Like the wings of some aeroplanes, the slots lessen the drag on the wing during soaring flight (see Aerofoil diagram).

In order to delay stalling, the wing tips of soaring birds have slots or spaces that are formed by the separation of the tips of the primary feathers. The slots permit air through from below — to maintain a smooth upper flow necessary for lift. An additional slot is provided by the alula, ('false wing' or 'bastard wing') located at the wrist of all birds.

Wing slots are minimised or absent in the high speed wing.

The flight feathers of owls are soft with 'fuzzy' posterior edges so as to muffle the sound of air as it passes over the feather. This feature equips owls with 'silent flight', and allows them to descend undetected on nocturnal prey. Additionally it permits them to keep their 'sound radar' tuned in on prey moving on the ground, without being confused by the noise of their own feathers. The flight feathers of fast raptors, such as the Peregrine Falcon, that catch prey in the air, tend to be stiff. Stiff feathers offer the ability of tight steering at high speed, a luxury afforded raptors that do not

49

Feathers require constant maintenance. A good shake ('rouse') after preening shakes off dust and realigns individual barbs of each feather.

normally risk feather breakage by engaging in ground tussles with their prey.

Feathers wear out and have to be replaced; therefore, all birds shed and periodically replace their feathers. This is called moulting. The moulting process of any bird is an orderly system, which only permits a few of the major flight feathers to be shed at any given time, so as to preserve the ability for flight. As soon as a pair of feathers (one from each side) are shed and replaced, an adjacent pair are shed and replaced, and so on, until the moult is completed. Raptors generally moult once a year. All raptors are covered with infant down when they first hatch from the egg. While confined to the nest, the chick's down is replaced by flight plumage within a matter of weeks. This plumage, known as immature plumage, is retained during their first year of life. It is nearly always (except for a few species of kestrels and most owls) different, both in colour and feather pattern from that of the adult. Some giant raptors, such as the large eagles, generally take more than one annual season to replace all their body feathers, and the immature plumage of the first year is no exception. For this reason eagles are categorised according to the feathers they display as immature, 'sub-adult' or adult, since it takes two years or more to form the adult plumage. The season for moulting, in all raptors, coincides with the spring and summer breeding season. Energy is required to grow new feathers; therefore, moulting occurs during the period of greatest food availability; and since moulting slightly impairs flying ability, it occurs during the period of easiest living.

Breeding and Reversed Sexual Size Dimorphism

All raptors generally breed in the spring and early summer when food availability is at a premium, and environmental temperatures favour the raising of young. All are monogamous and produce one set of young per year. Most raptorial species are solitary and prefer isolated nesting sites away from other pairs of the same species. Raptors which mainly feed on plentiful food such as insects or small rodents, require relatively small hunting territories, and may even be communal (kites, for example) in their feeding habits. Those species that feed on larger, often more evasive prey, require

immense hunting territories. Raptorial species which do not occupy the same ecological niche (compete with each other for food) may coexist peacefully within the same hunting territory.

Interestingly, all birds of prey display the phenomenon of reversed sexual dimorphism. The great majority of bird species exhibit sexual dimorphism, in which the male is slightly to considerably larger than the female. Within all birds of prey the exact opposite is true — females are slightly to considerably larger than the males. The exact reason is not eminently clear as to why nature designed this difference; however, several explanations exist. One suggests that among raptors the female needs to be dominant, to prevent undue harm to her during mating by the more sexually aggressive male. Another suggests that the male, being smaller and quicker, is the more efficient hunter and, therefore, able to provide better while the female incubates and cares for the young. A third suggests that the female being the largest and most aggressive, makes her the better choice for protecting the young against predators.

The above are just a few of the fascinating features displayed by birds of prey, and it is this fascination that has cemented the bond between man and raptor.

Right: The female (left) and male (right) Peregrine Falcon clearly display reversed sexual size dimorphism.

The Golden Eagle regularly migrates into the Gulf region from Europe and Central Asia, but it also breeds locally in mountainous regions.

FALCONS AND OTHER BIRDS OF PREY IN THE GULF

The hostility of the Gulf's 'hot season' has limited the number of raptors that reside as local breeders. Kestrels and Sooty Falcons have established residency, but the breeding status of larger falcons, with the exception of sketchy reports on the Barbary, is absent.

The local Barn Owl, Striated Scops Owl, Little Owl and Eagle Owl find the living fairly easy with their nocturnal feeding habits, and they commonly breed throughout the region. Egyptian and Lappet-faced Vultures are found year-round in the mountainous regions, and the Osprey along the rocky, coastal tip of Oman. The occasional buzzard and eagle are found to nest in the mountainous regions of Oman.

It is during the fall and spring that the coastal areas of the Arabian Peninsula present a veritable 'cornucopia' of raptor life. Most raptors find their way into Arabia as migrants from the more temperate climates of eastern Europe and central Asia, enroute to their wintering grounds in Africa. Two major migratory flyways converge to funnel migrants across the Peninsula. The first draws from Europe and the Baltic states and extends across the Mediterranean through Syria, Lebanon and the Red Sea. The second draws from the Caucasus, crossing through Afghanistan, Pakistan and Iran, then into the Gulf area before dispersing into Africa. From September through to November millions of birds, and the raptors that feed on them, move down the eastern and western coasts of the Arabian Peninsula.

The falcon and exotic bird markets extending from Riyadh to Lahore also contribute to the variety of raptor species in the Gulf. The strong regional influence of falconry has resulted in the creation of 'bird souqs' which promise to meet the seasonal demand for falcons. The souqs are supplied by wholesalers peddling their freshly trapped wares

MIGRATION CHART

The major migratory flyways of the western Eurasian Continent. The inserts show the record figures of birds of prey counted during one migratory season! Although no figures from the Strait of Hormuz are available, it is possible, that if there was an observation station in the Musandam, the record figure of over one million raptors counted during one season in Eilat, could easily be beaten. (These figures were obtained from the Swiss Institute of Ornithology in Sempach.)

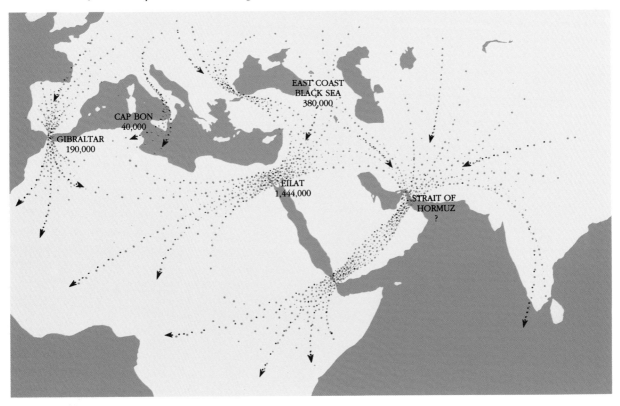

Although no numbers are available, the raptors listed below are known to migrate through the Gulf area, whilst the ones marked with an asterisk are recorded as resident breeders.

Peregrine Falcon
(*Falco peregrinus*)
* Barbary Falcon
(*Falco pelegrinoides*)
* Common Kestrel
(*Falco tinnunculus*)
Hobby
(*Falco subbuteo*)
Lanner Falcon
(*Falco biarmicus*)
Luggar Falcon
(*Falco jugger*)
Saker Falcon
(*Falco cherrug*)
* Sooty Falcon
(*Falco concolor*)
Western Red-footed Falcon
(*Falco vespertinus*)

Goshawk
(*Accipiter gentilis*)
Levant Sparrowhawk
(*Accipiter brevipes*)
Sparrowhawk
(*Accipiter nisus*)
Common Buzzard
(*Buteo buteo*)

Honey Buzzard
(*Pernis apivorus*)
* Long-legged Buzzard
(*Buteo rufinus*)

Dark Chanting Goshawk
(*Melierx metabates*)
Pale Chanting Goshawk
(*Melierx canorus*)

Hen Harrier
(*Circus cyaneus*)
Montagu's Harrier
(*Circus pygargus*)
Pallid Harrier
(*Circus macrourus*)
Western Marsh Harrier
(*Circus aeruginosus*)

Black-shouldered Kite
(*Elanus caeruleus*)
Black Kite
(*Milvus migrans*)
Brahminy Kite
(*Haliastur indus*)
* Osprey (Fish Hawk)
(*Pandion halieatus*)

* Bonelli's Eagle
(*Hieraaetus fasciatus*)
Booted Eagle
(*Hieraaetus pennatus*)
Golden Eagle
(*Aquila chrysaetos*)
Spotted Eagle
(*Aquila clanga*)
Lesser Spotted Eagle
(*Aquila pomarina*)
Imperial Eagle
(*Aquila heliaca*)
Pallas' Fish Eagle
(*Haliaeetus leucoryphus*)
* Short-toed Eagle
(*Circaetus gallicus*)
Steppe Eagle
(*Aquila nipalensis*)

* Egyptian Vulture
(*Neophron percnopterus*)
Griffon Vulture
(*Gyps fulvus*)
* Lappet-faced Vulture
(*Aegypius tracheliotus*)

Barn Owl
(*Tyto alba*)

* Eagle Owl
(*Bubo bubo*)
* Little Owl
(*Athene noctua*)
Long-eared Owl
(*Asio otus*)
Scops Owl
(*Otus scops*)
Short-eared Owl
(*Asio flammeus*)
* Striated (Bruce's) Scops
Owl (*Otus brucei*)

from vast regions. These regions extend from Syria, India, Afghanistan and Iran and run along the Gulf of Oman to the south of Yemen. Consequently, foreign raptors (those that migrate by a different flyway, or non-migratory raptors that are indigenous to another geographical region) will frequently find their way into the region. Additionally, Arab falconers have shown a recent interest in the large, northern, non-migratory falcons, and specific hybrids of these falcons that are being bred in Europe and North America. Therefore, the wealth of raptors found in the Arabian Gulf region draws on local breeding residents, the vast migratory flyways which draw from eastern Europe, western and central Asia; the bird souqs which occasionally provide non-indigenous raptors, and the relatively recent captive breeding endeavours of western countries.

A beautiful Saker/Gyrfalcon hybrid produced through captive breeding.

The classification of birds of prey

It is possible for confusion to exist over exactly what constitutes a bird of prey. For instance, if all meat eating birds were raptors, then cormorants, gulls, frigate birds, crows, ravens, magpies and countless others would have to be included. Yet if birds that only killed and ate others were classified as raptors, then vultures would have to be excluded. Therefore, in the simplest and broadest terms, a raptor can be defined as a carnivorous bird, with a sharply hooked beak designed for tearing flesh, that feeds wholly or chiefly on meat taken by hunting.

Confusion also exists as to how raptors are grouped, especially when comparisons are made between scientific taxonomy and the terminology of falconry. Much of the latter is an arcane lexicon which can be incongruous with scientific or lay definitions. For example, is a falcon a hawk or vice versa? If you train a bird of prey to hunt for you, does it become a falcon? If falcons are a large family of raptors with specific characteristics, why are only the females called falcons by traditional falconers? And so on. Most Arab falconers, in contrast to western falconers, do not attribute significance to any raptor other than falcons and, therefore, tend to categorise raptors into two or three large groups — those that are of intense interest to them, the large falcons, and 'others'. 'Others' may constitute a hawk or 'baz' group and a large 'shomalia' or eagle group (regardless of whether they are eagles, large kites or vultures). For further discussion of falconer's jargon, both Arab and western, refer to chapter 2. The scientific classification is the one of sense and significance.

Taxonomy is the science of grouping living things according to shared anatomical, physiological and related ancestral characteristics. A taxonomic example begins with the largest group, all sharing the most common characteristics, and progresses by means of subdivisions to the smallest group sharing the most characteristics. Obviously the starting place would be at the kingdom level, which divides into two major groups — plant and animal.

Kingdoms are divided into phyla. The animal phylum we are interested in is Chordata — animals with the foundation for a vertebral column (birds, mammals, etc.). Phyla are divided into classes.

The class consisting of birds is known as Aves (backboned animals with feathers). Classes are

CLASSIFICATION OF BIRDS OF PREY

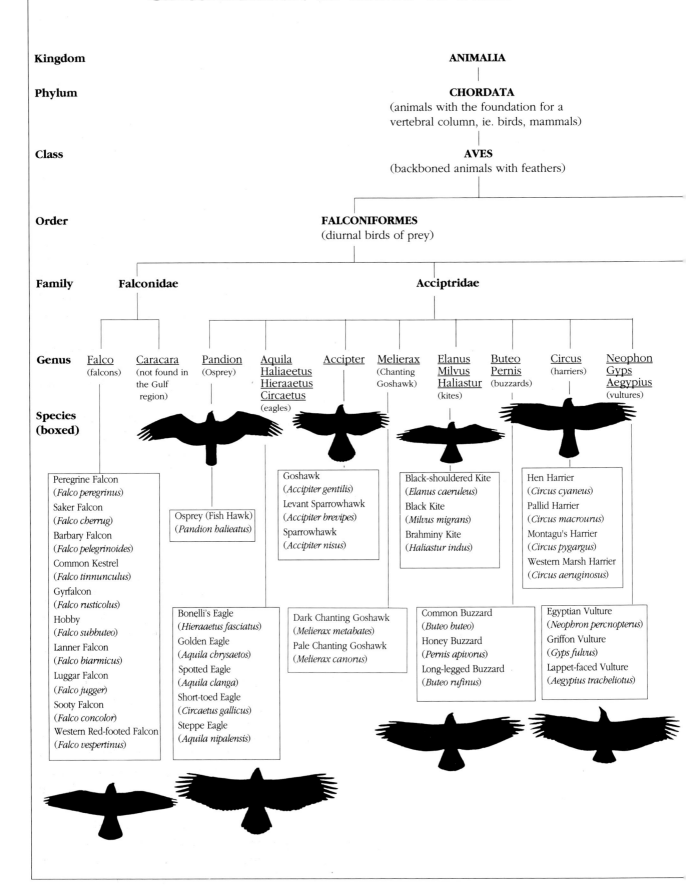

Kingdom — **ANIMALIA**

Phylum — **CHORDATA**
(animals with the foundation for a vertebral column, ie. birds, mammals)

Class — **AVES**
(backboned animals with feathers)

Order — **FALCONIFORMES**
(diurnal birds of prey)

Family — Falconidae — Acciptridae

Genus —
Falco (falcons)
Caracara (not found in the Gulf region)
Pandion (Osprey)
Aquila Haliaeetus Hieraaetus Circaetus (eagles)
Accipter
Melierax (Chanting Goshawk)
Elanus Milvus Haliastur (kites)
Buteo Pernis (buzzards)
Circus (harriers)
Neophon Gyps Aegypius (vultures)

Species (boxed)

Peregrine Falcon
(*Falco peregrinus*)
Saker Falcon
(*Falco cherrug*)
Barbary Falcon
(*Falco pelegrinoides*)
Common Kestrel
(*Falco tinnunculus*)
Gyrfalcon
(*Falco rusticolus*)
Hobby
(*Falco subbuteo*)
Lanner Falcon
(*Falco biarmicus*)
Luggar Falcon
(*Falco jugger*)
Sooty Falcon
(*Falco concolor*)
Western Red-footed Falcon
(*Falco vespertinus*)

Osprey (Fish Hawk)
(*Pandion halieatus*)

Goshawk
(*Accipiter gentilis*)
Levant Sparrowhawk
(*Accipiter brevipes*)
Sparrowhawk
(*Accipiter nisus*)

Black-shouldered Kite
(*Elanus caeruleus*)
Black Kite
(*Milvus migrans*)
Brahminy Kite
(*Haliastur indus*)

Hen Harrier
(*Circus cyaneus*)
Pallid Harrier
(*Circus macrourus*)
Montagu's Harrier
(*Circus pygargus*)
Western Marsh Harrier
(*Circus aeruginosus*)

Bonelli's Eagle
(*Hieraaetus fasciatus*)
Golden Eagle
(*Aquila chrysaetos*)
Spotted Eagle
(*Aquila clanga*)
Short-toed Eagle
(*Circaetus gallicus*)
Steppe Eagle
(*Aquila nipalensis*)

Dark Chanting Goshawk
(*Melierax metabates*)
Pale Chanting Goshawk
(*Melierax canorus*)

Common Buzzard
(*Buteo buteo*)
Honey Buzzard
(*Pernis apivorus*)
Long-legged Buzzard
(*Buteo rufinus*)

Egyptian Vulture
(*Neophron percnopterus*)
Griffon Vulture
(*Gyps fulvus*)
Lappet-faced Vulture
(*Aegypius tracheliotus*)

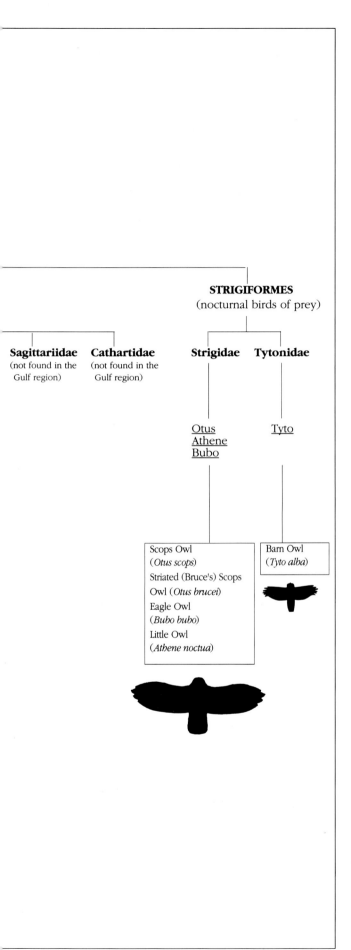

STRIGIFORMES
(nocturnal birds of prey)

Sagittariidae
(not found in the
Gulf region)

Cathartidae
(not found in the
Gulf region)

Strigidae   **Tytonidae**

Otus
Athene
Bubo

Tyto

Scops Owl
(*Otus scops*)
Striated (Bruce's) Scops
Owl (*Otus brucei*)
Eagle Owl
(*Bubo bubo*)
Little Owl
(*Athene noctua*)

Barn Owl
(*Tyto alba*)

further divided into orders. All orders end with "..iformes". The orders that contain the raptors are Falconiformes (diurnal birds of prey) and Strigiformes (nocturnal birds of prey, or owls). Orders, in turn, are further subdivided into families. All families end with "..idae". The families of diurnal birds of prey (not owls) are the Falconidae (falcons and Caracaras), Accipitridae (accipitrine hawks, kites, eagles, Ospreys, harriers, buzzards, accipiters and Old World vultures), Cathartidae (New World vultures) and Sagittariidae (Secretary Birds). The families Cathartidae and Sagittariidae are not represented in the Gulf. The next subgroup within a family is known as a genus. All the known genera of falcons, for example, occur within the family Falconidae. **Species** are subdivisions within a particular **genus**, which are composed of related organisms or populations potentially capable of interbreeding among themselves, but not with members of another species. A species is designated by a binomial that consists of the name of the genus followed by the latinised species name. The species name is not capitalised. A subspecies is a geographical variant or race of a particular species that is fully capable of breeding with any member of the parent species to which it belongs.

The following is a taxonomic example of the race of Peregrine Falcon found on the Indian subcontinent —

Kingdom	Animalia
Phylum	Chordata
Class	Aves
Order	Falconiformes
Family	Falconidae
Genus	*Falco*
Species	*Falco peregrinus*
Subspecies	*Falco peregrinus peregrinator*

Note that all subgroups from genus downward are italicised, and that the proper designation of a species must include the generic name, and that the proper designation of a subspecies must include the generic and species names.

The diurnal birds of prey occurring in the Gulf region are represented by two major families, the Falconidae and Accipitridae. The family Falconidae consists of the falcons and caracaras. Falcons represent the most specialised and highly evolved group of raptors. There is only one genus, *Falco*, with 39 known species worldwide. Within the falcon species, the circumpolar Gyrfalcons are the largest, Peregrine Falcons are the most cosmopolitan in distribution, and Merlins and Kestrels are the smallest. Caracaras do appear in the Arabian Gulf.

The Accipitridae family is comprised of Accipitrine Hawks, buzzards, chanting goshawks, harriers, kites, eagles, Old World vultures and Ospreys.

The Sparrowhawks and Goshawks are accipiters. They are small to medium-sized forest raptors, characterised by a dashing, shifty flight and an undaunting, reckless courage. Physically they possess relatively short, broad wings, long tails and long, powerful legs and feet.

Their hunting methods usually consist of a surprise attack from a familiar, secluded perch. Their non-hunting mode of flight consists of several quick wingbeats interspersed with short glides. When chasing other birds, their wingbeats become rapid and powerful, approaching gamebird-like proportions.

Buzzards, or buteonine hawks are generally large, broad-winged, soaring raptors, which primarily feed on rodents. Unsuspecting birds are occasionally taken by these large, beautiful, but somewhat undashing raptors.

Harriers are medium-sized raptors with relatively weak powers of flight. They have adapted themselves to low sailing, hovering and occasional flapping forms of hunting. They are birds of the marsh that prey upon snakes, lizards, insects, frogs and small mammals.

Kites are fairly primitive (in the evolutionary scheme), and are a relatively unspecialised group of medium to large-sized raptors with weakly developed feet and talons. They are soaring birds with weak powers of flight, and largely subsist on snails, insects and carrion.

The Osprey shares certain characteristics with sea eagles and buzzards. It has a worldwide distribution and mostly subsists on fish.

Eagles consist of three taxonomic groups — large fish or sea eagles, (which subsist on fish and carrion), Old World snake eagles (which are medium to large-sized raptors that primarily feed on reptiles) and the large booted eagles. Booted eagles possess feathered tarsi and feed on large mammals such as hares and marmots. Their slow but powerful wingbeat belies their speed, which enables them to catch and feed on large birds such as ducks and occasionally other raptors.

Vultures are large, soaring raptors that feed on carrion. Unlike most other raptors, vultures, especially New World vultures, have a better developed sense of smell, and relatively weak, 'non-rapacious' feet and talons.

The Strigiformes, or owls occurring in the Gulf region consist of two families — the Tytonidae (Barn Owls) and Strigidae. Owls are nocturnal avian predators which mainly feed on insects and small mammals. Barn Owls of the genus, *Tyto*, are cosmopolitan in distribution. Eagle Owls are the largest of the owls and are 'horned' with feathered ear tufts. They feed on a large variety of animals — including pet cats and the occasional, sleeping diurnal raptor. In Arabia, Africa, Europe and Asia, the Eagle Owl is the equivalent of the North American Great Horned Owl, while the Scops Owl, a miniature representative of the 'horned owls', is the equivalent of the North American Screech Owl.

Falcons

Since much of the subject of this book examines the cultural heritage of Arab falconry, and since falcons are essentially the only raptors used for this purpose by Gulf falconers (in fact the term 'falconry' derives specifically from their suitability for the sport worldwide), it is only fitting that major focus be given to this superbly specialised group of raptors. Falcons are muscular, compact, relatively long-winged, diurnal birds of prey which are included in a single genus, *Falco*. They range in size from 100 grams (the smallest kestrels) to 2 kilograms (the largest Arctic Gyrfalcons).

Falcons are distributed throughout the world and are found on every continent except Antarctica. The Peregrine is perhaps the best known species, and has a worldwide distribution. The Arabian Gulf region has no 'typical' breeding Peregrines, but several Peregrine subspecies pass through during migration — these include the Mediterranean (*Falco pereginus brookei*), Northern Russian (*Falco pereginus calidus*), European (*Falco pereginus peregrinus*) and several others. Smaller, Peregrine-like species such as the Barbary Falcon (*Falco pelegrinoides*), and possibly the Red-nape Shaheen (*Falco pelegrinoides babylonicus*) do breed in the Arabian Peninsula, but little is known of their whereabouts or density. Saker Falcons (*Falco cherrug*), the traditional favourite among Arab falconers, breed in eastern Europe and Asia, and are only migratory visitors to the Gulf.

It is interesting to note that many falcons have breeding areas that are geographically separate

The Peregrine Falcon is thought to be the fastest creature on earth. In a 'stoop' (dive) it has reached speeds in excess of 300 km/hour.

from the ones they occupy the rest of the year. Subtropical and tropical species tend to occupy the same areas year round, with little to no migratory wanderings. However, northern breeding species tend to migrate great distances to escape the harsh northern winters. For example, Arctic Peregrines of the western hemisphere migrate to South America, and those of the eastern hemisphere migrate to Africa.

There are many features that set falcons apart from other raptors. They display relatively short yet stocky beaks in comparison to head size. Their beaks are powerful and are used not only for eating but for killing captured prey. All falcons possess a unique structure on the cutting edge of the upper mandible known as a 'tomial tooth'. This tooth corresponds to a notch on the cutting edge of the lower mandible. It is thought that the tomial tooth assists in the disarticulation of the cervical (neck) vertebrae of captured prey. All falcons (with the exception of an African species that does not occur in the Gulf) possess a dark, chocolate-brown iris. The resulting rich, dark eye colour is present in both immature and adult falcons, and this darkness, unless viewed in bright light, can be confused with profoundly dilated pupils. The 'bella donna'-like appearance of a falcon's eyes undoubtedly is one of the captivating traits of the genus.

The feet of falcons, though formidable weapons, lack the vice-like crushing features of typical hawks and eagles, and their individual toes tend to be longer than those of other raptors. The characteristic pursuit and capture method of most falcons is a high speed dive culminating with the delivery of a glancing blow from the feet. It was always assumed that falcons delivered a blow with clenched feet, so as to minimise the risk of injury. However, slow motion photography has shown that a 'toes extended' strike is delivered with the rear talon raking across the area of impact. Just how damage to the feet is avoided, considering the speeds involved, remains a mystery.

Falcons have relatively long, pointed wings with moderate to stiff quilled flight feathers. Each wing has 10 primary flight feathers, and in most species the second outermost primary is the longest. In flight, most falcons exhibit a wing

Top: The Black Shaheen is a medium-sized dark peregrine subspecies that is non-migratory and breeds on the Indian Subcontinent.
Bottom: An adult female Red-naped Shaheen, a very close relative of the Barbary Falcon.

Pigeons are often used to exercise falcons in the early stages of training.

silhouette similar to that of a pigeon or duck, although the wing is portionately longer. The wingbeats of a falcon are also quicker and more powerful than that of a pigeon.

Wing loading is a term pertaining to the aerofoil of a wing. Birds with a broad wing loading, such as vultures, eagles, kites, harriers and buteonine hawks, use a soaring/searching method of hunting because their wings capitalise on the buoyancy of thermal air currents to keep them aloft. Large buoyant wings are usually clumsy, and raptors possessing them generally lack rapid acceleration. Accipitrine hawks, such as the Goshawk and Eurasian Sparrowhawk, display a light-wing loading, and their relatively short, grouse-like wings give them tremendous acceleration and turning ability.

Most falcons are heavy-wing loaded raptors — the larger the falcon, the heavier the loading. Although not as buoyant as large, broad-winged raptors, falcons are capable of fast, sustained flight and high manoeuvrability, which combine to make them successful aerial hunters capable of catching flying prey that would elude most other raptors.

Falcons are opportunistic hunters and primarily hunt by two methods — the 'stoop and glancing blow' or the mid-air 'chase and grab'. The method chosen by the falcon will depend on either the size, and elusive flight capabilities of the prey being sought, or the opportunity that presents itself at the time of the hunt. Large gallinaceous prey (pheasant, grouse, etc.) generally are faster in flight than a pursuing falcon, but speedy prey lack manoeuvrability. Therefore, the stoop is the most successful method for catching prey that would be capable of outflying a falcon. However, the highly manoeuvrable Houbara Bustard can easily elude a diving falcon with a simple dodge. Therefore greater flying speed will favour the falcon in an attack on the Houbara, and a series of spectacular chase and grab aerial manoeuvres will prove to be the successful method.

Falcons fly at incredible speeds. The Peregrine, which is the most versatile aerial specialist, probably flies at about 100 km/hr. The terminal velocity of the bird in a dive (stoop), however, is astounding, and makes it the world's fastest animal. The measured speed of a Peregrine's dive has been recorded at well over 320 km/hr.

The Arctic Gyrfalcon far outdoes the level flight speed of a Peregrine. Although slightly less speedy in a dive than the Peregrine, the Gyr is capable of sustained level flight at a speed of approximately 160 km/hr. This ability enables the Arctic Gyrfalcon to eventually catch ptarmigan grouse after long, exhaustive chases.

An adult Peregrine Falcon. This is the classic bird of falconry, and the overall favourite among falconers worldwide.

Although falcons are among the world's most successful predators, they spend much of their time hunting — largely because many of their hunting attempts end in failure. As with much that occurs in the animal world, the strongest and most cunning individuals are favoured. Falcons often prey on weak and sick animals. In times of plenty falcons will also prey on 'reproductive excesses', to maintain the natural ratio of predator and prey.

Inaccessible cliffs are the usual sites chosen by large falcons to hatch and rear their young. During the breeding season nesting sites are defended by the parents with a series of threatening dives and aggressive vocalisations. Young falcons are encouraged to leave the nest through food withholding by the parents. They are taught to hunt through observation, and mid-air transfers of dead or live prey during early flight education. When the young demonstrate an ability to feed themselves, they are abandoned and left to survive alone. They either quickly develop into capable hunters, or perish. Nature is harsh; only one-third of the falcons born during a given year survive to see their second year.

Peregrine Falcon (*Falco peregrinus*)

Identification: *Adult* — The feathers of the head and neck are sooty black with a heavy moustachial or 'malar' stripe extending down from the eye; cheek patches, throat and underparts are white to sienna orange, narrowly striped on the chest and barred on the belly. Their flanks are dark brown to black. The upperparts of the back and wings are slate-bluish grey barred with dark brown, and the flight feathers tend toward dark slate-brown barred with lighter slate-grey; the tail is tipped in white to beige. Skin of the cere, legs, feet and surrounding the eye (lore) is bright yellow to orange.

Immature — The head and neck feathers are dark brown with sandy streaking. The upperparts are also dark brown but have an amber feather edging. The tail is grey brown with lighter, amber spots and the face and underparts are white to sandy brown with dark brown streaking. Skin of lore, cere, legs and feet is blue progressing to greenish-yellow as the bird approaches adulthood.

Peregrines are stocky, heavily muscled, streamlined falcons. Size (measured from beak tip to tail tip) ranges from under 12.5 centimetres for the smallest tropical males, to over 48 centimetres for the largest females. Similarly, their weights range from 450 grams to 1,200 grams.

Description and Distribution: When most people think of a falcon they evoke the image of a Peregrine. Indeed the term 'falcon', in the lexicon of western falconers, historically refers to the female Peregrine, while the male is called 'tiercel' because he is one-third smaller. The name means 'wanderer', and the species has the most extensive distribution of any bird in the world. They do not nest above 4,000 metres, and they do not occur on the continent of Antarctica, but they are found in scattered distribution anywhere there is adequate territory to meet hunting requirements. Peregrines prefer a close proximity to water, and similar to other falcons, Peregrines are opportunistic hunters. Their diet includes tiny songbirds to geese and herons, although pigeons and doves are the preferred food items.

Present estimates place the global population of Peregrine Falcons between 12,000 and 18,000 breeding pairs. The population consists of 22 subspecies — most of which have been produced through geographical isolation. The largest subspecies breed in the arctic Aleutian Islands, while the smallest breed in tropical climates.

Peregrines are among the swiftest and most

*The Peregrine Falcon has the most extensive
distribution of any bird in the world.*

powerful fliers, and their aerial manoeuvres are awe-inspiring. J. A. Hagar (in Bent's *Life Histories of Birds of Prey*) colourfully illustrates this in his description of the courtship flight of the male, "...again and again he started well to the leeward and came along the cliff against the wind, diving, plunging, saw-toothing, rolling over and over, darting hither and yon like an autumn leaf until finally he would swoop up into the full current of air and be born off on the gale to do it all over again... Nosing over suddenly, he flicked his wings rapidly 15 or 20 times and fell like a thunderbolt. Wings half-closed, he shot down past the north end of the cliff, described three successive vertical loop-the-loops across its face, turning completely upside down at the top of each loop, and roared out over our heads with the wind rushing through his wings like ripping canvas. Against the backdrop of the cliff his speed was much more apparent than it would have been against the open sky...We felt a strong impulse to stand and cheer."

The Saker Falcon is probably the most versatile Houbara hunter and therefore the favourite among Arab falconers.

Saker Falcon (*Falco cherrug*)

Identification: *Adult* — There is probably more variation in plumage coloration and marking within this species than any other species of falcon. The majority of sakers tend to have buff underparts which are streaked, blobbed or spotted with darker shades of brown. Feather markings on the chest and flanks resemble an immature Peregrine except they are courser, less orderly and more heavily streaked. Head coloration is buff streaked with brown, but the marking varies — fine streaking confers a 'blond' appearance to the crown and nape, whereas the heavy markings are similar to those of the immature Peregrine. The malar stripe is absent or weak. The upperparts range from light tan (typical of 'blond' birds) to slate grey-brown (typical of the *altaicus* subspecies). Saker feathers are marginated and marked with buff to lighter brown. Tail coloration conforms to the upperparts, but the marking varies The skin of the feet, lores and cere is yellow.

Immature — The plumage colour and marking is similar to adult Sakers, only lighter and 'dustier' in appearance Feathers of the upperparts are marginated with cream to buff, and are uniformly dusty-brown (not marked). Skin of the feet, lores and cere is light blue.

Description and Distribution: Saker Falcons also greatly vary in size. Males average 38.5 centimetres in length with a wingspan of 91 centimetres, and weigh between 700 and 990 grams. Females average 47 centimetres in length, with an average wingspan of 108 centimetres, and weigh between 970 and 1,300 grams. Sakers are generally smaller than Gyrfalcons in both weight and body size, even though in proportion to body size they tend to have longer wings. Sakers tend to be larger than Peregrines, but size is deceptive since they are not as compact (this increase is more a reflection of overall length and not mass).

Many authorities feel there is some overlap between Sakers and Gyrfalcons. The so-called 'Altai Falcon' of the Asian mountains presents the strongest evidence. The Altai may represent a natural hybridisation between the Saker and Gyrfalcon that has become a separate species through geographical isolation; however, it is probably a large, dark subspecies of Saker (*Falco cherrug altaicus*). Interestingly, the Altai Falcon was the favourite of Attila the Hun.

In the wild, Sakers mainly feed on small mammals, although birds and reptiles are also

The Altai Saker (Falco cherrug altaicus) was previously thought to be a natural hybrid between the Gyrfalcon and the Saker occurring in the Altai Mountains of Asia.

hunted. Most prey is taken on the ground; therefore, they tend to be far less aerial than Peregrines. Hunting is primarily accomplished by low 'searching' flights.

Nesting sites range from the abandoned stick nests of other birds to cliff ledges. Sakers have an extensive nesting range which extends from eastern Europe throughout Asia — from the Baltic States of Czechoslovakia and Hungary to Turkey, Russia and as far east as Mongolia. Sakers are weak migratory birds compared to Peregrines; however, major flyways do carry large numbers from eastern and Mediterranean Europe, Asia and Pakistan to the Middle East and North Africa. Some travel via the Nile River into the Sudan, Ethiopia and Kenya.

This large, soft-feathered, hearty desert falcon is the traditional favourite of Arab falconers. Sakers are sluggish compared to Peregrines, but they are aggressive, rough and tumble hunters when trained. A willingness to engage in ground combat with large quarry, and an ability to withstand the harsh desert environment, makes the Saker, among all falcons, the best-suited falcon for Arab hawking. In Northern Africa, Sakers have even been used to hunt small gazelle in conjunction with coursing salukis. The Saker will harass the gazelle until it is confused, and slowed enough to allow the salukis to move in and finish the job.

Barbary Falcon (*Falco pelegrinoides pelegrinoides*) and Red-naped Shaheen (*Falco pelegrinoides babylonicus*)

Identification: *Adult* — Plumage shows the general coloration of the Peregrine, only paler on the upperparts and less heavily barred on the underparts. The desert Barbary is the palest, with only traces of barring on the underparts. African and Arabian Barbary Falcons display symmetrical, rufous patches on the nape of the neck, which are relatively conspicuous against the sooty, streaked, Peregrine-like crown and collar. The differences between the Red-naped Shaheen and Barbary Falcon are subtle — Red-napes display a more ferruginous crown, blending into a streaked, rufous nape. The feather margination of the upperparts is cinnamon or rufous, and the breast and flanks are sparsely barred. The Asian Red-napes are larger, yet less stocky than African and Middle Eastern Barbaries.

Immature — Both types of falcon share certain characteristics. Their plumage is similar to immature Peregrines, only paler and more amber. Unlike immature Peregrines, the skin of the cere, eyes and feet is bright yellow-orange, like the adults. Their size ranges from 29 centimetres to approximately 40 centimetres and their body weights from 360 to 730 grams.

Description and Distribution: There is a great deal of debate regarding the classification of these medium-sized, desert falcons. Attempts have been made to reclassify both as diminutive, desert subspecies of the Peregrine; however, the original classification of *Falco pelegrinoides pelegrinoides* for the Barbary Falcon, and *Falco pelegrinoides babylonicus* for the Red-naped Shaheen are favoured.

The little 'shaheen falcons' of North Africa, the Middle East and central Asia constitute an interesting and overlapping complex. In particular, the Barbary resembles a miniature Peregrine, with an exaggeration of the Peregrine's most classic features.

Both sexes display a proportionately more massive pectoral girdle and sternum than Peregrine Falcons. Their feet are larger and most specifically, the males display a proportionately longer wing length and shorter tail than Peregrines. Apart from a general stockiness, the Barbary Falcon and Red-naped Shaheen have a light wing-loading, which makes them more aerial.

There is a large degree of reverse sexual dimorphism amongst these species — the males are slightly more than half the size of females. The wing length however, is almost 85% of the female's.

The breeding range of Barbary Falcons extends from the African Barbary Coast across northern Africa and into Arabia. Little has been documented regarding their whereabouts or density in Arabia; however, they occur in scattered distribution throughout Saudi Arabia, where habitat will support them. They are relatively common in the Yemen and mountainous regions of Oman. The 'known' limits of the Red-naped Shaheen extend from western Turkey, throughout Afghanistan, Iran, Pakistan and into parts of Tibet. They may overlap with true subspecies of Peregrine, and even occupy the same ecological niche (hence the confusion with Peregrine); however, both the Barbary and Red-naped Shaheen appear to be geographical variants of a distinct desert race, for nowhere in the world have Peregrine Falcons evolved a specific desert form.

Similar to Peregrine Falcons, the little Red-naped Shaheen primarily feeds on prey taken in flight, and their preferred food items appear to be doves and pigeons.

A handsome adult female Barbary Falcon. Owing to its classic falcon features, the Barbary has been described as the 'beau ideal' of what a falcon should be.

Common Kestrel (*Falco tinnunculus*)

Identification: *Adult* — Most adult Kestrels exhibit sexual dichromatism. The male has a dove-grey head and black streaked nape. The tail is grey to slate-blue, and terminally marked with a single, broad band of black. The upperparts of the back are sienna and V-spotted with dark brown. The underparts are cream, V-spotted and finely streaked with brown. The female is less colourful, being more uniformly brown on the head and tail. The tail is finely barred with a number of dark brown bands and is tinged with grey.

Immature — The male Kestrel resembles the adult but has a grey tail tinged with sienna. Female Kestrels have more heavily barred tails which do not display the grey tinging of the adult. The underparts of male are heavily spotted, while the female's are heavily streaked.

Description and Distribution: The Common Kestrel is a small to medium-sized falcon with a wingspan averaging about 75 centimetres, and a relatively long tail. The body weights range from 170 to 200 grams.

This falcon has a breeding and residential range second only to the more cosmopolitan Peregrine — it is found throughout every major land mass within the Eastern Hemisphere, except Australia and Antarctica, and is believed to have the largest

The Common Kestrel is one of the most adaptable birds in the world. It is a local breeder in the Gulf.

population of any raptor species in the world. Its success relates to its adaptability, as is demonstrated in the fact that Kestrels inhabit most types of environments. It is a common year-round resident of the United Arab Emirates.

Its success further relates to its wide and varied diet, which consists of earthworms, snails, insects, lizards, snakes, small mammals, bats and small to large birds. Most Kestrels focus their attention on the ground in their search for prey. As with most kestrel species, 'hovering' and 'still hunting' are common methods of hunting.

Gyrfalcon (*Falco rusticolus*)

Identification: *Adult* — There are three recognised colour phases of this large Arctic Falcon — white, grey and 'black' (dark grey). However, these colours range from almost pure white on the underparts of some birds with fine black markings on the upperparts, through to various shades of grey-brown; including the so-called 'silvers' to a sooty slate-grey (resembling Altai Sakers) on the dark falcons. Plumage of the adult bird is barred like Sakers. The malar stripe is absent in white birds and weak in dark birds. The colour of the feet, lores and cere is yellow.

Immature — The overall markings are similar to juvenile Saker and Peregrine Falcons. However, during the maturation process the hues of each colour phase tend to be much browner in the immature birds. For example, immature white Gyrfalcons are heavily marked with light to medium brown, and the dark phases see the birds heavily marked with sooty chocolate-brown. Skin of the feet, lores and cere is bluish white.

Description and Distribution: The Gyrfalcon has the distinction of being the largest falcon on earth. Its size follows the ecological principle that the most northerly located species is the largest. Measurement from beak to tail tip ranges from 46-53 centimetres. There is a large degree of sexual dimorphism. Males average about 1,000 grams, and weights of 2,100 grams have been recorded for very large females (most range between 1,550 and 1,700 grams). Body conformation resembles a Saker, only Gyrs tend to be stockier. Wing length is short in proportion to body length, and the length of the folded wing characteristically extends only half to three-quarters of the way down the tail.

The climbing power and flying speed of the Gyrfalcon is unequalled. As stated previously the Gyr is capable of a level flight of 160 km/hr.

Adult female Red-naped Shaheen. Their resemblance to
Barbaries, can confuse identification, particularly where
breeding ranges overlap.

Gyrfalcons are thought to be a close relative of Saker Falcons, and as such their hunting methods are similar. Prey species include lemmings, Arctic hare, ptarmigan, waterfowl and other large birds.

Gyrfalcons are weak migratory birds and only move to less harsh northern climates in winter. Their breeding range is circumpolar, generally extending above the 60-degree meridian from upper Alaska to Greenland in the Western Hemisphere, and from Scandinavia to Siberia in the Eastern Hemisphere.

Their speed, power and large size make them attractive to Arab falconers; however, being Arctic falcons, they are poorly adapted for long-term survival out of their natural habitat. From both physiological and immunological standpoints, even the healthiest Gyrfalcons rapidly succumb to common temperate climate pathogens, that under normal circumstances would only be a nuisance for a healthy Saker or Peregrine. Gyrfalcons quickly perish upon direct exposure to the midday desert sun.

The speed and size of the Arctic Falcon makes it attractive to Arab falconers; however, the bird's health suffers greatly in the heat of the Gulf, and most quickly perish.

The miniature Hobby is one of the most aerial of falcons.

Hobby (*Falco subbuteo*)

Identification: *Adult* — The upperparts are dark slate coloured, and the underparts are heavily streaked with black on buff. The thighs and under tail coverts are rufous. The head is Peregrine-like with a black nape, crown and malar stripe, and light cream to white cheeks and throat.

Immature — Is similar to the adult, has a light feather edging on the back. There is very little sexual dimorphism — males weigh 130-230 grams, while the females weigh 140-300 grams. The body length is 30-35 centimetres.

Description and Distribution: The little Hobby is one of the most acrobatic falcons. It is a swift, long-winged, long-tailed falcon, smaller than the Common Kestrel, and relatively more buoyant than a Peregrine. Its diet primarily consists of flying insects (such as dragonflies) and small birds. Prey is usually snatched midair, on an upward swoop after a fast level flight or stoop.

The breeding range stretches from the British Isles, across Europe and northern Asia to Japan. The Hobby is almost exclusively a tree nester; therefore, they are found in heavily wooded areas. They commonly use the abandoned stick nests of other birds. Hobby Falcons migrate into southern Africa and India, hence they have a transient appearance in the Gulf during autumn and spring.

Lanner Falcon (*Falco biarmicus*)

Identification: *Adult* — The body plumage is similar to the Peregrine's, only lighter. In contrast to the distinct barring of the Peregrine, the markings of the underparts are more blotched or blobbed. The main distinction is the head — the crown and nape is reddish-buff, and the malar stripe relatively weak. The desert Lanners resident to Arabia and Northern Africa, are pale on top, with little barring on the back.

Immature — The body plumage resembles that of an immature Peregrine, only lighter and more buff. The crown and nape tend to be yellow-buff.

Description and Distribution: Lanners are Peregrine-sized falcons but slighter in build and lighter in wing-loading. Their wingspan measurements range from 90 centimetres in males, to 120 centimetres in females. Their body weights range from 500 grams to 850 grams. The Lanner prefers desert or semidesert regions, and nests on cliffs or bluffs. Its diet consists of small to medium-sized birds, small mammals, reptiles and insects.

The Lanner is a peregrine-sized desert falcon. Owing to their light wing-loading they are very aerial; however, they lack the power and speed of the peregrine.

The Luggar Falcon is thought by some taxonomists to be the Indian equivalent to the African Lanner Falcon.

Luggar Falcon (*Falco jugger*)

Identification: *Adult* — The general appearance of the Luggar's plumage is rather unremarkable — uniformly brown on the wings, back and tail, with cream to buff underparts streaked with brown. Only the outer tail feathers have light barring. The crown has a cinnamon to ferruginous tinge streaked with darker brown. The malar stripe is weak.

Immature — The plumage is similar to that of the adult, but the underparts are solid brown. The tail feathers are unbarred.

Description and Distribution: The Luggar's body measurements range between 35-40 centimetres, and weighs from 500 to 720 grams. Its flight is buoyant and kite-like. They are often confused with a very 'slight' or light-bodied male Saker Falcons; however, the feet are less muscular and the toes are slender and relatively weak.

Luggars nest in open desert areas on rocky outcrops or occupy abandoned stick nests in trees. They prey on small to medium-sized birds, but will also scavenge. As Luggers have a poor reputation as falconry birds, they are often used by falcon trappers as 'barak hawks'. (See 'Capture of falcons')

71

The Sooty Falcon is a resident of the Gulf Islands near Bahrain and Abu Dhabi.

Sooty Falcon (*Falco concolor*)

Identification: *Adult* — As the name suggests, the Sooty's plumage is uniformly sooty. Adults occur in two colour phases — a light, uniform grey, and a melanistic (darker) slate brown-grey. The primaries are charcoal grey and without markings.

Immature — Coloration of the plumage is a sooty brown. The back is brown, with a light buff margination on the feathers. The underparts are buff, and streaked with brown. There is a malar stripe below the eye. Sooty Falcons are slender, and measure between 32.5-35 centimetres. Sexual dimorphism is not very pronounced — the males are about 90% of female size. Their body weights range from 298 to 340 grams.

Description and Distribution: Most of these small falcons are island nesters, and are resident in North Africa, the Red Sea and the Arabian Gulf. They are common in the Gulf of Oman and the Howar Islands south of Bahrain. Being gregarious raptors they tend to nest in scattered groups. They primarily feed on small birds, insects and bats. Sooty Falcons migrate to West Africa and Madagascar at the end of the nesting season.

Western Red-footed Falcon (*Falco vespertinus*)

Identification: *Adult* — As the name suggests, these falcons display bright orange-red skin coloration of the lores, cere and feet. The Red-footed Falcon exhibits little sexual dimorphism, but does have the unusual feature of sexual dichromatism (male and female plumage are different colours). The males are dark sooty grey on the upperparts, with rich chestnut brown thighs and bellies. The upperparts of the female are blue-grey, barred with black (like a Peregrine). The underparts, crown and nape of the female are orange-buff, blending to cream on the cheeks. Both sexes have a moustacial or malar stripe below the eye.

Immature — Both sexes resemble the adult female, but are streaked with black on the head and nape. Feathers on the upperparts are marginated with amber-brown. The underparts are buff, heavily streaked with dark brown. The skin of the feet is bright yellow.

Description and Distribution: These are small falcons — about the same size of a male Hobby. Their weights range from 150 to 170 grams. These birds breed in north-eastern Europe and Russia. Stick nests taken over from other birds or holes in trees are the preferred nest sites. They are gregarious falcons that tend to hunt in colonies. This falcon is a trans-equatorial migrant that winters in South Africa. Its appearance in the Gulf is strictly migratory.

The tiny Western Red-footed Falcon migrates across the equator into South Africa.

Other birds of prey

The Hobby is almost exclusively a tree nester.

This large group comprises the remainder of the raptors, including the owls, that occur in the Gulf. The massive Accipitridae family contains 223 species, but for this chapter, only the species represented in Southern Arabia will be considered.

When one examines the vast diversity between the groups within the Accipitridae, it is hard to imagine how a Griffon Vulture could be more closely related to a Black-shouldered Kite than to a Condor; nevertheless it is. As mentioned earlier, taxonomic grouping is based on shared anatomical, physiological and related ancestral characteristics. Recently this family has been restructured into 13 categories, based on possible evolutionary relationships.

Accipitrine Hawks

A major sub-group within the Accipitridae family are the short-winged, woodland hawks known either as Accipitrine Hawks, the Accipiters or in falconer's terminology, 'short-wings'. Accipiters are not resident anywhere within the Gulf; they only make an appearance during migration.

This is a highly specialised group of raptors, superbly adapted to catching large or small-winged birds and mammals. These prey species live in relatively dense cover, an environment that does not favour the hunting style of a falcon. Their dashing speed, lightning-fast turning ability and reckless courage has made them favourites among falconers worldwide. As described in chapter one, the accipiters have played a major role in the sport of hunting with raptors from ancient times, up to, and including the present. As they are adapted to flight in areas of 'wooded cover', their hunting techniques are quite different from those of most falcons. The techniques and methods by which they are trained also differ substantially from those of falcons — so much so that the trainer of a short-winged hawk is more properly referred to as an austringer than a falconer. So efficient are accipiters at catching certain prey, that during medieval times Goshawks were often kept for the purpose of providing game meat for the table.

In areas where quail abound, the Sparrowhawk has always been a favourite among falconers. Many birds, including quail, 'explode' from cover to cover and thus escape most raptors. To catch them with Sparrowhawks, falconers trained their birds to lie horizontally in the palm of their hand, waiting to be 'thrown' javelin style at the quarry. A leather strap called a halsband was often attached to the hawk's neck, so that it could be 'catapulted' towards the quarry. Today, as in the past, the Goshawk remains the favourite among Japanese falconers. There is a large and growing group of accipiter devotees in North America. And accipiters are still trained and flown extensively throughout Europe and Asia — including India, Pakistan, Iran, Turkey and Syria.

Accipiters possess powerful, relatively short, rounded, gallinaceous-type wings (pheasant, grouse, etc.), relatively long tails, long-reaching legs and powerful, grasping feet. The wing shape and quick wing-beat confers an acceleration that is unparalleled among other raptors. The long tail offers instant braking and sharp-turning ability.

Goshawk (*Accipiter gentilis*)

Identification: The head is dark brown to black with conspicuous white eyebrows. The base of the nape feathers is white, tipped with black, which gives a white, mottled appearance to the neck. The feathers of the back, wing and tail coverts are slate-grey. Flight feathers of the wings and tail are grey-brown. Primaries and tail feathers are heavily barred with dark brown to black, and the tail is tipped in white. The forehead, cheeks, throat and underparts are white to ivory. These areas are distinctly barred with black. The eye colour of the adult bird is orange. Skin of the feet and cere is bright yellow. Immature birds also show distinct white eyebrows, and unlike the grey upper surface plumage of the adult, the young birds show medium to cinnamon-brown plumage streaked in ivory to buff. The wings and tail are more distinctly barred with dark brown and the tail is boldly tipped in white. The underside is white to light cinnamon, heavily streaked to blobbed with dark brown. Eye colour of the juvenile birds is yellow (typical of all accipiters). The legs and feet are also yellow. There is a strong reversed sexual dimorphism with the birds ranging between 45-60 centimetres in size.

Description and Distribution: Hunting methods of the Goshawk consist of 'still hunting' from a secluded perch followed by a sudden, dashing, twisting and turning chase. When seen in the open, non-hunting flight usually consists of a few wing-beats interspersed with short glides.

Their preferred nesting and hunting habitat is the coniferous forest. Large stick nests are constructed in Conifers, Birch or Aspen trees. Goshawks are almost always seen near running water — where prey species tend to congregate. Their diet is varied — H. Bruell observed a pair of Goshawks over a 10-year period and found their food remains to consist of hare, domestic cats, rabbits, squirrel, weasel, small rodents, pheasant, partridge, pigeon, Shrike and Buzzard! Goshawks occur all across the temperate zones of the northern hemisphere; from North America, across Europe, Asia, China and Eastern Siberia. Primarily, they are a northern species. They are distributed well above the arctic circle, but their southern limits extend only as far as Spain, the Aegean Region and Turkey. The Goshawks that occur as migrant visitors to the Gulf probably come from Turkey.

The Goshawk is the largest accipiter.

Sparrowhawks have been trained as hunters throughout Asia and the northern Middle East.

Sparrowhawk (*Accipiter nisus*)

Identification: The Sparrowhawk is a miniature version of the Goshawk; however, they differ slightly in that the sexes show different coloration (sexual dichromatism) and there is a marked reversed sexual dimorphism. The male is light to dark grey on the head and back, with a darker tail that is heavily barred in black. The face of the male shows amber brown on the cheeks; cinnamon streaked with brown on the throat, with the remainder of underparts being white barred with dark grey-brown. The female is browner (less grey) above, with whitish cheeks, throat and eyebrows. The underparts are white, and noticeably more barred with dark grey-brown. Juvenile Sparrowhawks are similar to juvenile Goshawks, only they are barred on the underparts and not streaked. Their eyes are yellow in both the adult and immature birds. Males average a length of 27.5 centimetres and large females often exceed 37.5 centimetres. The largest group of the species is found in Northern and Central Asia.

Description and Distribution: Despite its small size, the Sparrowhawk is a fierce and courageous hunter that pursues quarry into the densest undergrowth. It preys mainly on small birds, but when the opportunity presents itself the Sparrowhawk will attack larger birds. This small Accipiter is a popular falconry bird. These little hawks are widely distributed throughout Europe and Asia. Those that migrate to the Gulf in winter probably come from Turkey.

Buzzards or Buteonine Hawks

The buteos and sub-buteos, or Buzzards as they are commonly known, constitute a very large group of raptors within the Accipitridae that, for the sake of simplicity, have been combined as the Buteonine hawks. When one thinks of a hawk, the image of a Buzzard or Buteonine hawk generally comes to mind.

These are large, broad-winged raptors that make themselves relatively conspicuous when they are present. In flight they are commonly seen soaring in thermal currents of air, and the wingbeats are slow but powerful. When perched they again make themselves conspicuous and often can be seen on the end of a branch or atop a telegraph pole or simply standing in the middle of a cultivated field.

Most members of this group are powerful enough to catch and hold prey as large as rabbits or pheasants; however, their preferred diet consists of rodents, insects and snakes. Though often persecuted by unknowing people, the buzzard hawks are generally known as the "farmer's friends".

The common **Common Buzzard (*Buteo buteo*)** is only a scarce migrant winter visitor to the Gulf. The eastern subspecies of the Buzzard is sometimes referred to as the Steppe Buzzard.

The **Western Honey Buzzard (*Pernis apivorus*)** has only rarely been reported as a migrant visitor to the United Arab Emirates. Pale individuals can be easily confused with the Long-legged Buzzard.

Long-legged Buzzard (*Buteo rufinus*)

Identification: This bird has heavy legs, feet and beak, similar to a small eagle. It is streaked with chestnut to dark brown above. On the underside the bird varies from white with amber sides to the breast, flanks and thighs to solid amber-brown finely barred with darker brown to solid amber-brown. The unbarred tail distinguishes this species from the common Buzzard. The legs are slightly "trousered", which makes them appear longer. Skin of the legs and cere is yellow. Eyes are brown. The bird averages 60 centimetres in length.

Description and Distribution: Its large size places it midway between a typical buzzard and a Bonelli's eagle. Diet consists of small mammals, birds, insects, lizards and carrion. They often "still hunt" by dropping on prey from a convenient perch, but are also good gliders and soarers, and do hover occasionally.

As a good all-rounder, the Long-legged Buzzard is capable of surviving in the harsh environment of the desert and is a resident breeder along the Gulf coast. Its distribution ranges from Northern Africa, across the Arabian Peninsula deep into Central Asia. It appears, that when choosing their nesting sites, they again prove to be all-rounders, as they will nest on trees, rocks, as well as on the ground.

A Long-legged Buzzard.

The Pale Chanting Goshawk is not a true goshawk; the only resemblance lies in its plumage and body shape.

Chanting Goshawks

These raptors are members of the genus, *Melierax*, a unique and evolutionary primitive subgroup within the Accipitridae having evolved from the harriers. They are not true goshawks as their name would suggest, nor are they accipiters (of the genus, Accipiter); they only display a plumage resembling that of goshawks, and they only mimic the silhouette of a typical accipiter by the length and shape of the wings and tail and the length of the legs. Both species the **Dark Chanting Goshawk** (*Melierax metabates*) and the **Pale Chanting Goshawk** (*Melierax canorus*) occasionally appear in the Gulf.

Identification: Overall the Chanting Goshawk is a grey bird on the back that from a distance can easily be mistaken for a male harrier. The tips of the wings are dark brown to black, while the inner primaries and remaining wing feathers are light grey. There is a conspicuous white rump-patch, and the tail is barred white and grey. The leg shanks are long, and the toes are relatively short and weak. The body length averages 40 to 50 centimetres.

Description and Distribution: The calls consist of a series of melodious whistling and fluting sounds, hence its name. In the Gulf region they are considered vagrant, yet they are known to breed in the Yemen and Southwestern Arabia.

Female Pallid Harrier from Wadi Al Rheum farm near Medina Zayed.

Harriers

The harriers are a major subfamily of the Accipitridae. All members of this group belong to the genus, *Circus*. Harriers are slender, long-legged hawks with owl-like facial discs and small, compressed beaks. The shanks of the legs (tarsi) are featherless. In flight the wings appear rather long and pointed. The tail is relatively long. The important field identifying mark is the conspicuous white rump patch on the back at the base of the tail. In most of the harriers the females tend to be brown and white, and the males tend to be grey and white.

Harriers frequent marshes or swamps where they feed on mice, frogs and snakes. Flight is a slow, searching type, characterised by long periods of gliding interrupted with the occasional wingbeat. The head is often seen to move from side to side as the bird searches for food.

Harriers are only migrant visitors to the Gulf. Species that commonly occur during migration are the **Western Marsh Harrier** (*Circus aeruginosus*) and the **Pallid Harrier** (*Circus macrourus*). Species that have rarely been encountered in the Gulf are the **Hen Harrier** (*Circus cyaneus*) and **Montagu's Harrier** (*Circus pygargus*).

A female Marsh Harrier at Al Wathba.

*Above: Black Kite ready to steal sand partridge
from Lanner.*
Below: Brahminy Kite preparing to land.

Kites

The Kites comprise a major evolutionary sub-group of the Accipitridae. They are primitive, poorly specialised birds that have developed into scavengers. They feed on insects, snails, discarded fish and other carrion, and can frequently be found near rubbish dumps. In general they are very gregarious raptors, and where common are usually seen in the hundreds soaring, gliding, hovering, dipping here and there in their constant search for food. The **Black Kite** (*Milvis migrans*) though very common in Pakistan and India is rare in the United Arab Emirates. The **Black-shouldered Kite** (*Elanus caeruleus*) is resident in the Yemen but very rarely seen in the Gulf.

Brahminy Kite (*Haliastur indus*)

The Brahminy Kite is considered to have evolved from the group of raptors known as the harriers, which separates it from the other related kites. Single sightings were made in Dubai in 1986 and 1987 and one was brought to the Dubai Falcon Hospital having been purchased from the 'souq' in 1988. Like the other kites and the harriers, they are not suited to be trained as hunting birds.

Osprey (*Pandion haliaetus*)

An Osprey in a 'suburban' nest.

The Osprey is a subfamily of the Accipitridae consisting of one species.

Identification: Top of head and back dark brown to black; underside of body, wings and tail are white with brown speckling.

There is a prominent malar stripe extending from the beak across the eye to the nape. Back of the head is white. Feathers extend half-way down the shanks of the legs. Skin of feet and cere is bluish-grey. Eye colour is orange-yellow. The Osprey measures 48.5 centimetres in length and resembles a medium-sized eagle.

Description and Distribution: The Osprey feeds entirely on fish that are snatched from the surface of the water. Although averaging only three pounds in weight, this bird manages to retrieve fish up to four pounds. It is the only diurnal bird of prey that possesses two toes directed to the front and two to the back. The purpose is thought to aid in gripping slippery fish.

The Osprey is distributed worldwide with the exception of South America. It constructs huge stick nests on prominent rocks, in trees or on man-made structures. Due to its feeding habits, it can be found in the vicinity of fresh water lakes or sea coasts. It breeds in the Gulf coastal areas.

79

Eagles

Certainly the largest members of the Family, Accipitridae, occur amongst the eagles; however, not all eagles are huge, and a few are no larger than small buteonine hawks. Recently the eagles have been divided into four major groups — Harpy Eagles, Sea or Fish Eagles, Booted Eagles and Snake Eagles. The Harpy constitutes a tropical rain forest group which does not occur in the Gulf. The large Sea or Fish Eagles and the Booted Eagles are thought to have evolved from the harriers, while the Snake Eagles, are thought to have derived as a primitive off-shoot of the early, ancestral kites.

The Sea or Fish Eagles have only been recorded in the Gulf by the single sighting of a **Pallas' Fish Eagle** (*Haliaeetus leucoryphus*) near Ras Al Khaimah. Their nearest regular wintering area is Pakistan and India. The **Booted Eagles** are those with 'feather boots' extending down the tarsi to the feet. The representatives that have been recorded in the Gulf are the **Lesser Spotted Eagle** (*Aquila pomarina*), the **Spotted Eagle** (*Aquila clanga*), the **Steppe Eagle** (*Aquila nipalensis*), the **Imperial Eagle** (*Aquila heliaca*), the **Golden Eagle** (*Aquila chrysaetos*), the **Booted Eagle** (*Hieraaetus pennatus*), the **Bonelli's Eagle** (*Hieraaetus fasciatus*) and the **Short-toed Eagle** (*Circaetus gallicus*). Most occur in the Gulf as migrants. The Bonelli's Eagle and the Golden Eagle are resident breeders in the area.

Bonelli's Eagle (*Hieraaetus fasciatus*)

Identification: The bird is dark brown above with a lighter greyish mantle on the upper back. Wings and tail are pale ivory-grey, mottled and subterminally banded with brown. Tail has a heavy terminal band. Face is brown streaked with white. Underparts are white streaked with brown blobs becoming heavier in the flanks. Legs are trousered in white to buff. Immatures are amber-brown and white, striped with dark brown. Juveniles replace white parts with amber-brown.

Beak and talons are blue-black. Skin of the cere and feet is yellow. Eye colour is yellow. The bird measures 52.5-60 centimetres.

Description and Distribution: These medium-sized "booted" eagles appear more slender and hawk-like than those of the genus, Aquila. They also possess powerful, long-toed, accipiter-like feet. Because of their Accipiter-like characteristics they have been popular falconry birds in Asia and Africa where they are resident. These are versatile hunters that feed on small mammals, birds and reptiles. They often hunt in pairs. They are normally forest or forest-edge dwellers. They are distributed from southern Europe (Spain and the

The Bonelli's Eagle, a 'booted' eagle, is halfway between a large accipiter and a large eagle. It has been successfully trained as an efficient falconry bird.

Mediterranean) all across Asia to China, and across the Arabian Peninsula throughout most of the forested regions of Africa. It is weakly migratory, and it appears in the Gulf in winter. A few are thought to reside in Oman.

Golden Eagle (*Aquila chrysaetos*)

Identification: The overall plumage is medium to dark brown. The feathers of the head and the hackle feathers at the nape are suffused with amber and tipped with tan giving a golden sheen, hence the name. Feathering on the tarsi is slightly paler. The tail is marked with lighter thin bands at the base, but the tip of the tail is dark brown. The bird does not achieve full adult plumage until the fourth year. Birds of the second and third year have much lighter feathered tarsi, and the base of the tail is broadly banded with white. Juveniles (first year birds) are nearly black with the bases of the body feathers being white. Underside of the primary, secondary and tail feathers white at their bases and black at the tips. This gives the bird conspicuous white patches on the undersides of the wings and tail. Tail has a single broad dark brown band terminally.

The beak and talons are black. Skin of the cere and toes is yellow. Eyes are dark brown. One of the largest eagles, this impressive bird measures 75-90 centimetres from beak to tail tip.

Description and Distribution: Golden Eagles have a worldwide distribution that nearly rivals that of the Peregrine Falcon. In the Holarctic it reins supreme among the eagles with the largest individuals occurring in North America. In Europe and Asia it occurs from Scotland across Scandinavia, all across Siberia to Korea. Southernmost limit in North America extends deep into Mexico, and in the Eastern Hemisphere extends from the Mediterranean, including North Africa, through Turkey, Iran and across to China. It does not occur in Australia or South America.

Golden Eagles rank as the strongest, fastest and boldest of the "true eagles". The relatively slow wingbeat belies their speed. Prey consists primarily of mammals ranging in size from lemmings to marmots. Hares are the preferred prey, although young lambs, goats, ducks and geese may supplement the diet from time to time.

These birds build large stick nests on cliffs and in trees. The preferred nesting habitat is mountainous terrain. Although not widespread, this eagle does nest in the Arabian Peninsula.

This handsome, juvenile Golden Eagle came from a nest near Oman.

Short-toed Eagle (*Circaetus gallicus*)

The Short-toed Eagle (*Circaetus gallicus*) is the representative of the Snake Eagle group that occurs in the Gulf. It is a resident breeder.

Identification: From a distance it can be confused with an Osprey, but it has less eagle angled wings. Generally the bird is dark brown with white spots and speckling. From the chest upwards it becomes darker, and the owl-like head is speckled with various shades of brown. Back, upper wings and tail are brown. Wing and tail tips are dark brown to black. Skin of the cere, legs and feet is greyish-blue. The eyes are very large and a conspicuous, brilliant yellow. The bird measures only 65 centimetres, which places it among the smaller eagles.

Description and Distribution: The eagle utilises a searching and hovering method of hunting; therefore, soaring is not typical of this species. The diet consists primarily of snakes. It is a resident breeder in the area. Stick nests are constructed in trees and on rocky outcroppings. The bird is distributed throughout Southern Europe and Asia.

The Short-toed Eagle is a resident breeder in the Gulf.

The Steppe Eagle is now considered to be a darker race of Tawny Eagle and not a separate species as once thought.

Steppe Eagle (*Aquila nipalensis*)

Identification: Plumage is a dark chocolate brown on the back and undersides. The crown is marked with black, and the rest of the head and neck are streaked with cinnamon. Primaries, secondaries and tail feathers are weakly barred with cinnamon. Immature and juvenile plumage tends to be lighter with the corresponding chocolate and cinnamon being replaced respectively by cinnamon and ochre. Underparts are mottled with light ochre. Skin of the cere and feet is yellow. The eye colour is yellow. This is a mid-sized eagle measuring 62.5-70 centimetres.

Distribution: The bird can be found, as the name suggests, throughout the Steppes. Otherwise the breeding range is similar to that of the Spotted Eagle.

This immature Spotted Eagle will lose its white spots and become an overall dark brown in adult plumage.

Spotted Eagle (*Aquila clanga*)

Identification: The bird is dark brown above and below. The secondaries, upper and under tail coverts and the tail are tipped in white. Feathers of the lower tarsi are mottled in white. Immature plumage is more mottled in white on the breast, and the secondaries and tail feathers are barred. The skin of the cere and feet is yellow. The eyes are brown. This is a mid-sized eagle measuring 60-67.5 centimetres.

Distribution: The eagle is distributed from the Baltic States all across Russia into China. The southernmost limit of its breeding range extends into Pakistan. The bird is a winter migrant into the Gulf region.

Lesser Spotted Eagle (*Aquila pomarina*)

Identification: In the field it is very difficult to distinguish the Lesser Spotted Eagle from the Spotted Eagle. It is slightly lighter in colour, grey-brown rather than dark-brown which from a distance is not recognisable. The immature Lesser Spotted Eagle has fewer white spots on its plumage than the immature Spotted Eagle. On both birds the skin of the cere and feet is yellow, whilst the eyes of the Lesser Spotted Eagle are light-brown with a distinctive black iris. It is a small-sized eagle measuring 54-65 centimetres.

Distribution: It has the same distribution as the Spotted Eagle and is a scarce winter visitor to the Gulf region.

Old World Vultures

The old world vultures comprise a major group (sub-family) consisting of ten **genera** and 16 **species** worldwide. The species that occur in the Gulf are the **Eurasian Griffon** (*Gyps fulvus*), the **Egyptian Vulture** (*Neophron percnopterus*) and the **Lappet-faced Vulture** (*Aegypius tracheliotus*) of which the last two are resident breeders.

Vultures are generally large birds with long, broad wings that can span up to 2.5 metres and are ideal for soaring during long hours. The plumage of both sexes is usually similar, whilst unlike other raptors, males tend to be larger than females. Most vultures are dark-brown to black in colour, with the exception of the Egyptian Vulture which is not only predominantly white, but also by far the smallest of the locally occurring species.

In contrast to other raptors the feet of vultures are poorly adapted to grasping and holding prey and well-adapted to walking. Vultures are carrion eaters, by large, and must cover vast distances in their search for food. Soaring at fantastic heights they may be undetectable to the human eye, yet their refined binocular vision confers the ability to locate carcasses from these altitudes. Most vultures will not attack an animal before it dies; rather, they prefer to sit and wait for death to ensue. Until recently it was assumed that vultures possessed finely developed olfactory senses. This was one explanation to the gathering of vultures around a carcass. It is now thought that one vulture, having spotted a carcass, will descend in a manner that 'signals' others in the area to the location. Each vulture having witnessed the decent then flies in and descends in a similar manner, which in turn signals others, etc. Although their sense of smell may be better developed than other raptors, they still rely primarily on their acute vision for the location of food.

Despite their repulsive feeding habits, vultures spend a great amount of time with personal grooming (preening and sand bathing). The head and neck of vultures are featherless. This is a hygienic advantage to feeding from within the depths of a carcass. The length of the neck can be greatly extended for further feeding advantage. Vultures have a feathered collar type of "neck-band", which may act as a soilage barrier to the remainder of the body plumage. Vultures have huge crops and stomachs, which allows them to consume vast quantities of food during times of plenty. During lean times vultures have the capability to fast for days, and remarkably, their young do not suffer from daily fasting either.

The Egyptian Vulture is a resident breeder in the UAE.

Egyptian Vulture (*Neophron percnopterus*)

Identification: Adult birds are predominantly white on the back and chest with a slight yellowish tinge to the back of the neck. Undersides of the wings are white. Wing tips are black, and major flight feathers are black and white. Face is featherless with yellow skin. The beak is slender and yellow and ends in a black tip. The legs and feet are featherless, and the skin is flesh-coloured. The shape of the tail is wedge-like and consists of 14 feathers. With a length of only 57 centimetres, it is one of the smallest vultures.

The immature bird is dark brown to black. Skin of the face, legs and feet are bluish-grey. It is only after the fifth moult that the adult plumage is completely attained.

Description and Distribution: This bird is the least specialised feeder among the Gulf vultures, and it can often be found around rubbish dumps. It is a resident breeder in the United Arab Emirates with a well-established breeding colony at Jebel Hafit. These birds can be observed near the zoo in that vicinity where they scavenge in the open lion cages.

It is distributed from the Mediterranean region down into Northern Africa and across the Arabian Peninsula into Central Asia.

Griffon Vulture (*Gyps fulvus*)

Identification: This bird has loosely constructed feathers of buff to sandy-white, tan on the back. Secondaries are darker and primary feathers as well as tail are black. Head and very long neck are sparsely covered with filamentous to downy white feathers. Collar is buff. Breast is ochre streaked with white. Beak is yellow, cere is bluish-black, eyes are reddish-orange and the skin of the legs and feet are dark grey. It measures 88 centimetres in length; the wings are very broad with a wingspan of up to 2.5 metres. It is slightly larger than the huge Lappet-faced Vulture.

Description and Distribution: Amongst the large vultures, the Griffon is the only bird that is not dark in colour but light to red-brown, with only the underside of the wings being predominantly black. They are extremely gregarious birds and large colonies can inhabit the same cliff. Their mating calls consist most unromantically of grunting, hissing and whistling sounds. Throughout their distribution range, vast numbers of these birds can gather around large carcasses to feed. They then often spend the night there, even roosting on the ground, which is probably due to the vast quantities of food they have consumed.

Griffon vultures are rare migrant visitors to the United Arab Emirates. They breed from the eastern Mediterranean region through Turkey, Iran, Pakistan and India. They also breed in the mountains of the western Arabian Peninsula, but they do not occur on the Gulf side. They prefer mountainous habitat and nest in cliffs. Sightings in flight are infrequent as they soar at altitudes of 3,000 metres or more.

The Griffon Vulture has a wingspan of up to 2.5 metres.

A Lappet-faced Vulture having a sand bath.

Lappet-faced Vulture (*Aegypius tracheliotus*)

Identification: Head and neck are featherless, cere is bluish to pink, skin of the head tends toward reddish with skin folds (lappets) on the side of the head and upper neck. The beak is massive and yellow. Back, tail and wings are dark brown. The vulturine neck band is white blending to brown as it meets the body feathers. Upper chest is speckled brown and white, lower chest is brown. Feathers of the thighs are greyish-white and give the bird a 'trousered' appearance. Lower legs and feet are featherless, and skin of the feet is bluish-grey. At 88 centimetres in length it is the largest local breeding raptor.

Description and Distribution: A typical carrion eater, it soars at enormous heights covering vast distances in its search for food. They are usually seen in pairs, but at a large carcass several may gather to feed. These birds prefer to build huge stick nests in the tops of trees. The Lappet-faced Vulture is non-migratory, and its distribution is confined to Northern Africa with some scattering into the Arabian Peninsula.

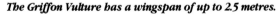

The Barn Owl is one of the most handsome nocturnal birds.

The Order Strigiformes

Owls

Owls are nocturnal birds of prey. Despite shared characteristics such as hooked beaks, grasping feet with well-developed talons and similar feeding habits, owls are not closely related to diurnal birds of prey. Fossil evidence traces the existence of owls back 70 to 135 million years. During the course of evolution nocturnal birds of prey developed into 133 species and became distributed worldwide. Two families exist and both are represented in the Gulf — *Tytonidae* is represented singly by the Barn Owl, and the family, *Strigidae*, is represented by the Eagle Owl, the Little Owl and the Scops Owl. All are resident breeders.

Owls have relatively short fan-shaped wings, rounded and vaulted at the tips, that allows a steady, slow flight. The legs and feet of most owls are covered, often to the beginning of the talons, with tiny hair-like feathers that act as silencers during flight and hunting. The feet of diurnal raptors are generally featherless, and have three toes directed forward and one directed to the back. By contrast, owls have two-toes directed forward, one directed back with the forth toe directed slightly backward and at a right angle to the adjacent fore toe. Among the diurnal birds of prey the Osprey is similar in that it has two toes directed forward and two backward which probably aids the bird in grabbing slippery fish while swooping over the water.

Owls castings in comparison to body size tend to be larger than those of diurnal birds of prey. This is because Owls normally swallow prey (mice and insects) whole and therefore, consume more indigestible matter than diurnal birds of prey. In the Gulf only the Eagle Owl is strong enough to kill prey which it cannot swallow whole. Another reason for larger casting pellets relates to the weaker acidity of gastric juices. The pH of stomach contents of owls is approximately 2.35 while that of diurnal raptors averages 1.6. Their digestive capability is less efficient requiring more indigestible material to be regurgitated.

After a night's hunt, food is digested during daytime. Owls are extremely territorial and the non-migratory breeding residents in the Gulf may use the same concealed roosts day after day for years. Therefore the floor beneath a roost can be littered with guano and the bones and insect shells of thousands of carcasses.

Barn Owl (*Tyto alba*)

Identification: A very light-coloured bird, chest almost white with some golden shades and 'jewelled' droplets marking the upper part. Wings, back and top of the head are golden brown to buff with some silvery grey spots. The two relatively huge facial discs are white and combine to form a heart-shaped face highlighting the well-defined round black eyes. Legs are finely feathered, the toes are feathered and the skin is bluish-grey. The bird's overall appearance depicts an elongated, rather slight long-legged body. There are no ear tufts. The Barn Owl measures about 30 centimetres in length; however, most of its size is made up of feathers.

Description and Distribution: It is a weak yet buoyant flyer. Hunting success is ensured by silent flight and phenomenal hearing. The Barn Owl preys solely on small rodents and insects. Insects are often caught searching on foot, while on its lookout for rodents, the Barn Owl prefers the 'perch-and wait' hunting method. From a perch, it searches the surroundings with ears and eyes. One perching area after another is tried until prey is located. Two mice per night may be all that is required to meet the dietary needs of the bird. Solely nocturnal in is activities and non-migratory, the Barn Owl is distributed over most of the temperate and tropical world, including Australia. Represented in the Middle East by the subspecies *Tyto alba erlangeri*, the Barn Owl follows civilisation as it prefers to inhabit old buildings which are a haven for small rodents.

A side view of a Barn Owl's head clearly shows the feathershield around its eyes.

Eagle Owl (*Bubo bubo*)

Identification: Buff to rusty brown colour, with dark to black bars on the wings, dark blobs on the upper chest and from the top of the head down the back to the tail. Large facial discs, light to buff in colour without markings. Eyes are large with prominent orange irises. Feathers cover leg shanks and dorsal aspect of the toes down to the origins of the talons. The prominent feather 'ear tufts' extending from the lateral margins of the facial discs give the owl an 'eared' or 'horned' appearance. With just under 50 centimetres total length (beak to tip of tail), it is by far the largest owl nesting in the Gulf.

Description and Distribution: Its size earns it the name, "Eagle Owl". It preys mainly on desert rodents and birds, but given the opportunity, it will also overpower baby gazelle, fox and hare. While hunting the Eagle Owl quietly glides just above the desert floor with only an occasional wingbeat. Hunting consists of 'searching' rather than a 'perch' method. They are not high soaring birds as height is a disadvantage to their mode of hunting. Furthermore, staying in ear-contact with the ground assists in the detection of prey.

The Eagle Owl's distribution ranges from Europe across the Asian continent to China and North Eastern Russia, and from Siberia to Northern Africa and the Arabian Peninsula. In this vast area it is represented by various, locally occurring subspecies. *Bubo bubo ascalaphus,* the subspecies of the Gulf, occurs throughout the whole of the Arabian peninsula up to Iraq and Syria and across Northern Africa. It breeds in holes on the ground, in cliff pot holes or it takes over abandoned stick nests from other birds. The Eagle Owl is very territorial, non-migratory and may occupy the same area for years.

The Juvenile Eagle Owl resting.

The Little Owl may be seen regularly during daytime.

Little Owl (*Athene noctua*)

Identification: Little Owls display a greyish-white chest streaked with brown spots. They are brown to greyish with white to light grey spots from the top of the head down the back to the tail, the wings are the same. Relatively inconspicuous greyish-brown facial discs are clearly framed under the chin by a pale collar and above the eyes by a white stripe extending down to the cere. Eyes are yellow. The head has no feather tufts, the legs and dorsum of toes are feathered. With its short tail it measures only 20-22.5 centimetres and belongs to the smallest group of owls.

Description and Distribution: The Little Owl may be seen in daytime, although its peak activity is at dawn and dusk. It feeds primarily on insects but also takes small rodents and reptiles such as geckos and lizards. It is mainly a 'perch and wait' hunter. The wings are short and rounded, flight over long distances is undulating. Like most owls it is territorial and non-migratory. The ancient Greeks described this owl, and it is thought to have been the favoured bird of the Goddess of Athens, hence its scientific name *Athene noctua*. The local subspecies is called 'Athene noctua saharae'. Little owls occur in Northern Africa, Europe, across Central Asia to Northern China and have been introduced into New Zealand. They are ground or tree dwellers and prefer to nest in hollows or holes in the ground. If disturbed they often disappear down a hole rather than fly away.

The Scops Owl is migratory and the subspecies seen in the Gulf are winter visitors.

Scops Owl (*Otus scops*)

Description and Distribution: There is some confusion between the Scops Owl and the Striated Scops Owl as both birds have the same appearance; however, the Scops Owl measures one inch shorter. The Scops is not a resident breeder in the Gulf. Its legs are also covered with feathers, but they do not extend onto the toes. Distribution ranges from Southern Europe across Central Asia to China. This owl is migratory, and the subspecies seen in the Gulf, *Otus scops turanicus*, are here only as winter visitors.

Striated Scops Owl (*Otus brucei*)

Identification: These owls are uniformly grey coloured with black streaks and slight brown shading on top of the wings as well as on the chest and the upper back. With folded wings, the tail is concealed giving the body a V-shaped appearance. The facial discs are inconspicuous, uniformly grey with fine black speckling. They have Large yellow eyes. Legs are short and feathered; feathering extends slightly down the toes. Prominent feather tufts on the head which are usually laid back and only visible when the bird becomes alarmed. The smallest of the breeding owls of the Gulf, the Striated Scops Owl only measures 18 centimetres in length.

Description and Distribution: A purely nocturnal bird, it starts hunting after dusk and feeds mainly on insects and the occasional small bird or rodent. The day is usually spent concealed on a tree branch. The Striated Scops Owl assumes an elongated appearance and with its colouring is so superbly camouflaged in its natural environment that at rest from a distance it may look like a broken branch. The Striated Scops Owl ranges from the Arabian Mediterranean Coast, across Lebanon, Syria, Iraq and Iran to Asia. The subspecies occurring in the Gulf, *Otus brucei exiguus* is both migratory (enroute to Africa) as well as resident. They prefer a habitat with small amount of vegetation and, therefore, can be found in and around cultivated areas. Like most owls they usually take over an abandoned nest or hole in a tree.

Threats, Accidents, Maladies and Future of Arab Falconry

Throughout the latter third of the twentieth century there has been an increasing awareness of man's impact on the environment and the wildlife within. In the West, and throughout most of the developed world, the precipitous decline of several species of raptors has alerted us to the dangers of non-degradable, insidious poisons that we were putting into the environment. Acknowledging and acting to avoid the threat to the survival of raptors and other wildlife will ensure the future of falconry thoroughout the world.

A major problem is the pesticide DDT. Unfortunate victims of its cumulative effects include the Osprey, several species of fish-eating eagles, bird-eating hawks, and the Peregrine Falcon. DDT causes a decrease in the thickness of eggshell, and as a consequence, eggs are either crushed under the weight of incubating mothers, or they undergo an excessive evaporative water loss, and the embryos die. This is a serious side-effect of 'high-tech' agricultural methods. Until this problem was recognised and there was a ban on DDT and DDT-like poisons in western countries, several species of raptors nearly became extinct. It is interesting today that in many underdeveloped countries, which do not have access to 'high tech' agricultural methods, raptor populations remain healthy. However, DDT is still in use to kill malaria-carrying mosquitoes and crop-eating insects, and has come into widespread use in overpopulated, developing countries. The raptors that were free of this threat before, may now be affected.

One of the more obvious ways that man destroys raptors is to shoot them. Raptors have been targetted by many gamekeepers, poultry farmers,

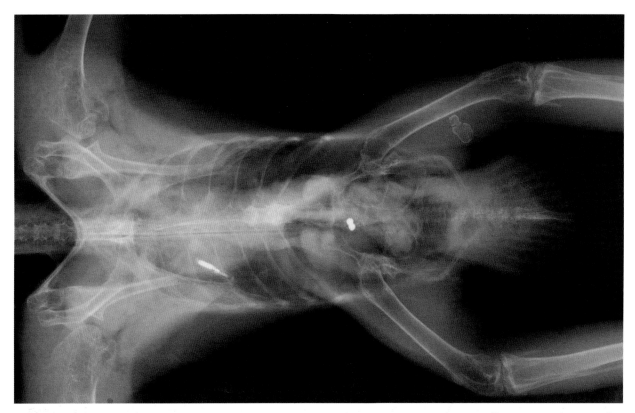

Lead poisoning is easily diagnosed. The lead shot imbeds in the lining of the stomach and slowly poisons the nervous system. The elongated object seen in the breast region is a harmless 'identification chip' which has been implanted under the skin.

pigeon fanciers and a few hunters — who simply cannot resist the temptation of shooting a big easy target. In spite of the laws protecting them, and the positive effect they exert in keeping rodent and pest populations in check, thousands of raptors continue to be slaughtered.

The increasing elimination of nesting habitat for both raptors and the prey species they feed on, has reached critical levels for many species. Most affected are the specialised birds and animals which are unable to adapt to changing conditions. Rain forest raptor species are a prime example. Fortunately, many species that would be thought to be endangered by natural habitat exclusion have surprised us with their 'adaptability'. The Peregrine Falcon is a classic example. In their natural habitat Peregrines require huge hunting expanses to satisfy their food needs, and tall, inaccessible cliffs to satisfy their nesting requirements. As more and more 'Peregrine areas' have given way to agriculture and human dwellings, many falcons have moved into the cities and taken up residence on skyscrapers, where they live off of the abundant populations of pigeons.

In Europe, many egg collectors endanger the lives of raptors. In a quest to complete their collections, most collectors are not deterred by the strict laws protecting raptors and their eggs.

Not only are raptors at threat within the environment, they also suffer a great number of mishaps. The vast majority of raptor accidents involve damage to the major flight, primary wing, and tail feathers. These feathers in particular, are relatively long and stiff, and their location exposes them to injury during tussles with large quarry. The loss of a single feather from each wing does not noticeably affect flight, but it does jeopardise the adjacent feathers; therefore, when a major feather breaks it must be repaired.

The process of feather repair is called imping. Feathers are repaired with an intrafeather shaft splint (otherwise known as an imping needle). Once they are fully grown and hardened, feathers are 'dead' appendages and have no nerves or blood supply. Therefore they can be cut at any point without any sensation registered by the bird. Unlike hair-growth, cut feathers do not grow back until the feather (stump) is dropped during the regular moulting period.

There are hundreds of diseases affecting raptors, and as this is not intended as a medical text, only the common, day-to-day pathological conditions seen in the Gulf will be mentioned. The most common complaint regarding a falcon's health is what Arab falconers refer to as 'dude'. Dude means worm, and specifically the worm (or two) that they are referring to is understandably the one they can visualise — most commonly a segment of a tapeworm, or rarely an entire roundworm. A 'heavy' infestation of tapeworms may cause a weight loss in a falcon, but in general, they cause little harm as most of the time only a small portion of the intestinal nutrients are stolen by the worm. It is impossible for one raptor to get tapeworms from another raptor. Tapeworms are easily ridded from their host with the aid of a single tablet taken orally.

Coccidiosis, known as 'cocc' in old western text books, is undoubtedly the most frequently diagnosed pathological parasitic infestation in the Gulf. Coccidia are microscopic protozoal (one-celled) parasites, similar in life-cycle and appearance to malaria, which occupy the cells of the intestinal lining. The completion of the parasite's life-cycle results in destruction of the intestinal cells, which in turn interferes with food absorption. Fortunately, this condition responds dramatically to a recently introduced coccidiocidal drug.

Trichomoniasis is one of the most well-known parasitic diseases in raptors. Accounts of 'canker' and 'frounce' (as it is more commonly known) can be found in the earliest records on the treatment of falcons dating back to the 9th century AD. The disease is caused by a protozoal parasite that lives in the upper digestive tracts of pigeons and other birds. A falcon most often catches the parasitic disease by eating an infected pigeon, and for this reason it is commonly referred to by local Arab falconers as 'the pigeon disease', or 'gurha fie lissan' (mouth canker). In Qatar and Kuwait this condition is referred to as 'glah'. The disease has fatal results, but fortunately it responds to modern trichomonacidal drugs, provided proper nutrition can be maintained during treatment.

Every animal has its own form of pox, and falcons are no exception. Pox virus in raptors causes lesions on the unfeathered skin of the feet,

A case of pox ('jidri') in an immature Peregrine Falcon. Though the scabs fall off within a few weeks, deforming scars occasionally result.

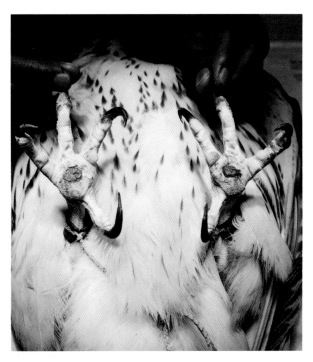

An advanced case of bumblefoot ('somar') in a falcon. Note the grossly overgrown talons, a major cause of the disease through self-inflicted injury.

cere and eyelids. In the Gulf region mosquitoes are the main source of infection; therefore, the disease shows a seasonal incidence. Most virus diseases, once they have gained entry, must simply run their course. But in the early stages of falcon pox — known locally as 'jidri' — the course can be shortened by drying the swollen, infected areas with an alcohol and mercurochrome solution, and by providing some vitamin supplementation.

Paramyxovirus infection or Newcastle disease is a virus disease that threatens birds throughout the world. This devastatingly contagious disease has caused enough damage to the poultry industry as to warrant the quarantine of all avian species coming into developed countries. The virus is spread between birds in the same way that influenza is transmitted among groups of people. The symptoms generally relate to the digestive tract, respiratory system and nervous system. Once the infection is contracted it is often fatal, and cannot be treated. Fortunately, there is a vaccine that confers protection against the virus for a year or longer.

Aspergillus fumigatus is a prevalent mould that causes one of the most common and potentially fatal diseases of captive raptors. It is a disease primarily of the respiratory tract, although not confined to it. Well known to Arab falconers, aspergillosis is referred to as 'hiatha' or 'redad'. The portal of entry for the fungus is the air; the spores are inhaled. Most birds normally harbour at least a few spores of *Aspergillus*; therefore, since the fungus is already present, the disease only tends to 'root' under conditions that weaken the immune system. A falcon with a healthy immune system will inhale millions of fungus spores with no ill effects. Prolonged stress will produce the disease in almost any raptor. An obvious period of susceptibility would be the time a bird first comes into captivity. If a falcon remains in a wild state for too long (this is stressful) or is made too thin for the purpose of training, that bird is also at risk of developing the disease. Another major cause of stress is prolonged, inescapable environmental heat. A large percentage of falcons kept over the summer and exposed to the heat of the Arabian Gulf, without the benefit of air conditioning, go on to develop this disease.

The most common bacterial disease condition seen in the Gulf is 'bumblefoot' or 'somar' as Arab falconers refer to it. The earliest medical description of the disease dates back to the 9th century AD. Bumblefoot is simply an infection of the foot caused by a *Staphylococcus* bacteria. The bacteria gains entry either through a puncture in the sole of the foot, caused by a talon, or by devitalisation of the skin barrier to infection. The most common devitaliser is bruising irritation that results in the formation of a 'corn'. The corn places compression on the sole of the foot, which impairs circulation and causes skin death. When a scab forms the bacteria are already well-established in the foot. The presence of the scab on the weight-bearing surface is also a barrier to healing, as healthy tissue cannot grow under and around the scab to mend the break. The condition is treated by surgery. Prevention is always the best medicine, and is easily accomplished by checking for the presence of early corn build-up with frequent examination of the falcon's feet, and by assuring that the falcon has a daily bath. The talons should also be checked so that they do not puncture the sole of the foot.

Captive falcons are best kept on a natural diet. However, a totally natural diet is difficult and illegal for a falconer to duplicate, as it contains many different varieties of protected birds. Most falconers feed their falcons on a natural diet consisting of pigeons, young chickens or captively raised quail. When a falcon eats a bird it utilises the bones of that bird to satisfy its demand for calcium. The falcon also benefits from the vitamins that are stored in the liver and gut of the prey. Without access to selected anatomical parts of a prey species, deficiencies quickly develop. However, the 'shot-gunning' of doves and pigeons as a natural food source for falcons has converted that food source into a potential poison. The tiny lead shot is eaten with the meat, but it does not pass out of the stomach. Slowly lead is released into the blood. The main targets of lead are the liver, bones and nervous system. The shot can often be removed with the feeding of several whole dead birds or mice. The casting or pellet that is produced from the feathers or fur, with a little luck, will often scour the lining of the ventriculus or stomach, and work the shot loose so that it can be trapped and packaged within the pellet. When the pellet is ejected the following day, it is washed and inspected for the presence of lead shot. If no lead is found the procedure is repeated.

Many Arab falconers, in their insistence to feed a natural diet, have tried to escape any associated problems by using nickel-coated lead-shot. Unfortunately, this is not the solution. The nickel coating cracks on impact as it enters the bird, thus exposing the lead, and the digestive juices act as efficiently at digesting the nickel as they do the lead. The only realistic solution to achieve a safe, natural diet is to feed falcons on pigeons, chickens or quail that have been raised specifically for the purpose.

A new generation of Arab Falconers.

The final issue to be discussed is the future for falconry, and in particular, Arab falconry. In the West, particularly in North America, it seems likely falconry will survive. The sport has 'come under the gun' countless times by well-intentioned but misinformed groups. At present, laws have been created to assure that both raptor and game populations will not suffer the slightest impact whatsoever as a result of falconry. In their crusade to keep their sport alive and well, western falconers have accepted and comply with regulations that most other hunting groups would consider excessive.

The laws and regulations that have assured the survival of the sport in the West are not the issue for the practice of falconry in Arabia. By comparison with the west, there are few regulations, and this can operate to the detriment of falconry in the long run. It is not the number of raptors that are at risk in Arabia. If DDT and related chlorinated hydrocarbon insecticides do not raise problems again, in this part of the world, raptor populations will probably remain stable for a long time. The only real issue that could halt Arab falconry would be a threat to the primary quarry of Arab falconry, the Houbara Bustard itself!

It has been stated numerous times in the previous chapters that Arab falconers have no interest in hawking any quarry other than the Houbara

Bustard, Stone Curlew and Arabian hare (where it is still legal to hunt it). The Houbara is the main quarry, and traditional Arab falconry techniques and training methods centre on catching it. Eliminate the Houbara and Arab falconry goes with it!

Well-known ornithologist, Dr Tom Cade, states in his book, *Falcons of the World*, "The Arabs want their birds to go straight to the mark and take the quarry as quickly as possible, because [they want to] catch as many head as possible." Consequently, "... there has been an alarming decrease in the numbers of Houbara Bustards in the last ten years, a fact which Arab falconers fully recognise. In part this reduction appears to have been brought about by man-induced changes in habitat on the breeding grounds, but it is hard to escape the conclusion that these bustards have been severely over-hunted in their wintering quarters, particularly when automatic shotguns are used in conjunction with falcons. Shooting has recently been banned in several Arab countries, and there is growing interest in programs to propagate Houbara for release to the wild..."

The recent interest in propagating Houbara for release to the wild demonstrates concern for the species and Arab falconry. Whether captive propagation would ever be successful enough to counter the present hunting pressures is doubtful. Of far greater promise and significance is the development of conservation measures involving the recreational hunting of wildlife. There is evidence to support temporary, selective hunting restrictions on the Houbara (not a ban per se, but limits on the numbers that could be taken), could indeed preserve the species. A prime example of the positive effects of hunting regulations was the enactment of a ban on hunting the Arabian hare in the United Arab Emirates (this species had been over-hunted to the point of near extinction). The ban apparently has been respected by the majority of the local people, as the hare is beginning to make a comeback. Therefore, it would appear that what is needed most to address the concerns of Arab falconry is a slight modification in attitude — an emphasis more on the 'quality of flight' than the day's 'head count'.

Changing conditions may now dictate that the true heroes of Arab falconry are not the men who at the end of the day have the largest number of dead Houbara, but the men who have shown the wisdom of leaving some for tomorrow.

Stone Curlew. This is one of the species that suffered a steady decline over recent years.

A Saker on the Gulf shores.

GLOSSARY

English	French	German	Latin
Accipitrine Hawks	Accipitridés	Habichtartige	Accipitridae
American Golden Plover	Pluvier doré asiatique	Kleiner Goldregenpfeifer	Pluvialis dominica
Arabian Hare	Lièvre du Cap	Kaphase	Lepus capensis
Arctic Tern	Sterne arctique	Küstenseeschwalbe	Sterne paradisaea
Barbary Falcon	Faucon de barbarie	Berber-oder Wüstenfalke	Falco pelegrinoides
Barn Owl	Chouette effraie	Schleiereule	Tyto alba
Black Kite	Milan noir	Sehwarzmilan	Milvus migrans
Black Shaheen	Faucon pélerin noir	Schwarzer Wanderfalke	Falco peregrinus peregrinator
Black-shouldered Kite	Faucon blanc	Schwarzflügel-Gleitaar	Elanus caeruleus
Black Vulture	Vautour moine	Mönchsgeier	Aegipius monachus
Bonelli's Eagle	Aigle de Bonelli	Habichtsadler	Hieraaetus bonelli
Booted Eagle	Aigle botté	Zwergadler	Hieraaetus pennatus
Brahminy Kite	—	Brahminenweih	Haliastur indus
Bustards	Outarde	Trappen	Otididae
–Arabian	Outarde arabe	Arabische Trappe	Ardeotis arabs
–Houbara	Outarde houbara	Kragentrappe	Clamydotis undulata
Caracaras	Caracaras	Karakaras	Polyborinae
Chestnut–bellied Sandgrouse	Ganga à ventre châtain	Braunbauch-Flughuhn	Pterocles exustus
Chukar	Perdrix chukar	Steinhuhn	Alectoris chukar
Common Buzzard	Buse	Bussard	Buteo buteo
Dark Chanting Goshawk	Autour chanteur	Graubürzel-Singhabicht	Melierax metabates
Doves	Tourterelles	Turteltauben	Streptopelia
- Collared	Tourterelle turque	Turkentaube	Streptopelia decaocto
- Palm	Tourterelle maillée	Palmtaube	Steptopelia senegalensis
- Rock Dove	Pigeon biset	Felsentaube	Columba livia
- Turtle	Tourterelle des bois	Turteltaube	Steptopelia turtur
Eagle Owl	Grand duc	Uhu	Bubo bubo
Egyptian Vulture	Perctoptère d' Egypte	Schmutzgeier	Neophron percnopterus
Francolin-Grey	Francolin gris	Grauwachtelfrankolin	Francolinus pondicerianus
Golden Eagle	Aigle doré	Steinadler	Aquila chrysaetos
Goshawk	Auttour des palombes	Habicht	Accipiter gentilis
Griffon Vulture	Vautour fauve	Gänsegeier	Gyps fulvus
Gyrfalcon	Faucon gerfaut	Gerfalk	Falco rusticolus
Hen Harrier	Busard Saint-Martin	Kornweihe	Circus cyaneus
Hobby	Faucon hobereau	Baumfalk	Falco subbuteo
Honey Buzzard	Bondrée apivore	Wespenbussard	Pernis apivorus
Houbara	Outarde houbara	Kragentrappe	Clamydotis undulata
Imperial Eagle	Aigle impérial	Kaiseradler	Aquila heliaca
Kairowan	Oedicnème criard	Triel	Burhinus oedicnemus
Kestrel	Faucon crécerelle	Turmfalk	Falco tinnunculus
Lanner Falcon	Faucon lanier	Lannerfalk	Falco biarmicus
Lappet-faced Vulture	Vautour oricou	Ohrengeier	Torgos tracheliotus
Lesser Spotted Eagle	Aigle pomarin	Schreiadler	Aquila pomarina

Levant Sparrowhawk	Epervier à pièds courts	Kurzfangsperber	Accipiter brevipes
Little Owl	Chouette chevêche	Steinkauz	Athene noctua
Long-legged Buzzard	Buse féroce	Adlerbussard	Buteo rufinus
Luggar	Faucon laggar	Laggarfalk	Falco jugger
Long-eared Owl	Hibou moyen duc	Waldohreule	Asio otus
Marsh Harrier	Busard harpaye, -des roseaux	Rohrweihe	Circus aeruginosus
Merlin	Faucon émerillon	Merlin	Falco columbarius
Mocking Bird	Merle moqueur	Spottdrossel	Mimus polyglottus
Montagu's Harrier	Busard de Montagu, -cendré	Wiesenweihe	Circus pygarcus
Nightjar	Engoulevents	Ziegenmelker	Carpimulgidae
Osprey	Balbuzard fluvatile	Fischadler	Pandion haliaetus
Pale Chanting Goshawk	Autour chanteur	Singhabicht	Melierax canorus
Pallas' Fish Eagle	Pygargue à queue blanche	Bindenseeadler	Haliaeetus leucoryphus
Pallid Harrier	Busard pâle	Steppenweihe	Circus macrourus
Peregrine Falcon	Faucon pélerin	Wanderfalk	Falco peregrinus
Ptarmigan	Lagopède muet	Alpenschneehuhn	Lagopus mutus
Quail — common	Caille des blés	Wachtel	Coturnix coturnix
Red-footed Falcon	Faucon kobez	Rotfussfalk	Falco vespertinus amurensis
Red-naped Shaheen	Faucon de Barbarie	Rotnackenschahin	Falco pelegrinoides babylonicus
Saker Falcon	Faucon sacre	Würgfalk	Falco cherrug
Sand Partridge	Perdrix de Hay	Arabisches Wüstenhuhm	Ammorperdix heyi
Scops Owl	Hibou petit duc	Zwergohreule	Otus scops
Short-eared Owl	Hibou brachyote	Sumpfohreule	Asio flammeus
Short-toed Eagle	Circaète Jean-le-Blanc	Schlangenadler	Circaetus gallicus
Sooty Falcon	Faucon concolore	Schieferfalk	Falco concolor
Sparrowhawk	Epervier d'Europe	Sperber	Accipiter nisus
Spotted Eagle	Aigle criard	Schelladler	Aquila clanga
Steppe Buzzard	Buse variable	Falkenbussard	Buteo buteo vulpinus
Steppe Eagle	Aigle des steppes	Steppenadler	Aquila nipalensis
Stone Curlew	Oedicnème criard	Triel	Burhinus oedicnemus
Whip-poor-will	Engoulevent bruyant	Pur-Will	Caprimulgus vociferus

PICTURE CREDITS

INDEX

BIBLIOGRAPHY

Allen, M: *Falconry in Arabia*, Orbis Publishing Ltd, London (1982)

Burton, S R: *Falconry in the Valley of the Indus*, John Van Voorst, London (1951)

Cade, T: *Falcons of the World*, Cornell University Press, Ithaca, New York (1982)

Chamerlat, C A de: *Falconry and Art*, Southby's, London (1987)

Freeman and Salvin: *Falconry, Its Claims, History and Practice*, London (1985)

Gallagher, M & Woodcock, M: *The Birds of Oman*, Quartet Books, London (1980)

Gensbol, B: *Collins Guide to the Birds of Prey of Britain and Europe, North Africa and the Middle East*, Collins, London (1984)

Glasier, P: *Falconry and Hawking*, Charles T Bradford Co, Newton Centre, Massachusetts, USA (1978)

Grossman, M L & Hamlet, J: *Birds of Prey of the World*, Clarkson N Potter Inc, New York (1964)

Grzimeks, Tierleben DTV: *Vogel*, Vol 7-9, (1968)

Heinzel, H, Fitter, R and Parslow, J: *Pareys Vogelbuch* (1983)

Hollom, P A D, Porter, R F, Christensen, S, and Willis, I: *Birds of the Middle East and North Africa*, T & A Poyser Ltd, Staffordshire, UK (1988)

Johnsgard, P A: *Hawks, Eagles and Falcons of North America*, T and A D Poyser Ltd, Staffordshire, UK (1990)

King, A S & McLelland, J: *Birds, Their Structure and Function*, Bailliere Tindall, Philadelphia, USA (1984)

Newton, I: *Birds of Prey*, Merehurst, London (1990)

Richardson, C: *Birds of the United Arab Emirates*, Hobby Publications (1990)

Schmid, H: *Greifvogel und Eulen* (1990)

Silsby, J: *Inland Birds of Saudi Arabia*, Immel Publishers, London (1990)

Tardif, G: *Livre de L'art de fanconnerie et des Chiens de Chasse*, Anthoine Verard, Paris (1492)

Wood, C A: *The Art of Falconry*, Stanford University Press, CA (1943)

ACKNOWLEDGEMENTS

Dr Remple is particularly grateful to His Highness Sheikh Hamdan bin Rashid Al Maktoum, whose support of the Dubai Falcon Hospital has highlighted his interest in falconry. Sheikh Hamdan has provided the opportunity to experience Arab falconry both in Pakistan and the UAE, and his friendship and support are cherished. This author also thanks HE Sheikh Hasher Al Maktoum and HE Sheikh Butti Al Maktoum for their assistance in translations with the text and for many enjoyable hours in the desert.

Christian Gross is particularly grateful to Sheikh Ahmed bin Mohammed Hasher Al Maktoum for providing him with an introduction to Arab falconry. He has been a source of valued tutelage, experience and friendship.

Both authors also wish to thank the Dubai Falcon Hospital staff, particularly Clayton Smith, M Abdul Majeed and Nigel Barton, who helped provide important photographs.

Khalifa Saif was particularly helpful in providing pictures gathered throughout his many years as a falconer in Abu Dhabi and has proven to be a great comrade over the years. In the same vein we would like to thank the Schweizer Vogelschutz (SVS) who were instrumental in obtaining required pictures at the last minute.

We would fondly like to remember Fred Brooks, a good friend who is missed and Muriel his wife, a friend still.

And finally, we would like to express our gratitude to EPPCO, whose sponsorship has made possible the publication of this book.

THE AUTHORS

David Remple, DVM

Dr Remple was born in Colorado, USA in 1942, and was introduced to falconry at the age of 13 by one of the founding fathers of North American falconry, the late Professor Robert M Stabler. He obtained a degree in zoology from the University of Colorado and later completed Veterinary Medicine at Colorado State University. Following veterinary college and a two-year term in the United States Air Force, Dr Remple ran a private veterinary practice in Wyoming, where he remained for the next nine years. During that time, he was a consulting veterinarian to the world renowned Peregrine Fund, whose aim was the restoration of the DDT-decimated Peregrine Falcon population in the United States.

Dr Remple has authored several manuscripts on raptor diseases and pioneered research into new treatment methods for raptors. In 1983 he was invited by His Highness Sheikh Hamdan bin Rashid Al Maktoum to found the Dubai Falcon Hospital — the first of its kind in the Middle East. He is Director of that facility and is assisted by his wife Cheryl, who is the Administrative Director of the Dubai Falcon Hospital.

Christian Gross

Swiss naturalist Christian Gross was born in Venezuela in 1957. He has accompanied his family on excursions into the South American jungle as well as visited South American Indian tribes. During his childhood in Switzerland, he learned the art of taxidermy in the Natural History Museum, Basel. After finishing his studies in business administration and later compulsory military service, he set out to pursue what he describes as an 'obsession in life' — travelling — while working aboard a ship.

Arriving in Dubai in 1979, he was fascinated by the harsh mountains and desert, and sought to document the wealth of wildlife he found there. He has bred local wildcats in captivity and cared for local breeds of snakes, fish, flamingoes, owls, eagles and foxes. In 1985 he was sponsored by HH Sheikh Mohammed bin Rashid Al Maktoum to conduct a survey of the mammals of Dubai. This survey led him to write *Mammals of the Southern Gulf*, which was published by Motivate Publishing in 1987. He has flown falcons in the desert of Dubai and also joined local friends on hunting trips to Pakistan.

In 1988 he returned to Switzerland, where he currently lives.

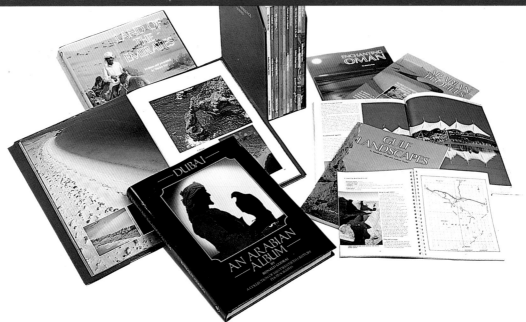

Arabian Profiles
edited by Ian Fairservice
and Chuck Grieve

Land of the Emirates
by Shirley Kay

Enchanting Oman
by Shirley Kay

Bahrain – Island Heritage
by Shirley Kay

Kuwait – A New Beginning
by Gail Seery

Dubai – Gateway to the Gulf
edited by Ian Fairservice

Abu Dhabi – Garden City of the Gulf
by Peter Hellyer and Ian Fairservice

Fujairah – An Arabian Jewel
by Peter Hellyer

Portrait of Ras Al Khaimah
by Shirley Kay

Sharjah – Heritage and Progress
by Shirley Kay

Architectural Heritage of the Gulf
by Shirley Kay and Dariush Zandi

Emirates Archaeological Heritage
by Shirley Kay

Seafarers of the Gulf
by Shirley Kay

Gulf Landscapes
by Elizabeth Collas and Andrew Taylor

Birds of Southern Arabia
by Dave Robinson
and Adrian Chapman

Falconry and Birds of Prey in the Gulf
by Dr David Remple and Christian Gross

Mammals of the Southern Gulf
by Christian Gross

The Living Desert
by Marycke Jongbloed

Seashells of Southern Arabia
by Donald and Eloise Bosch

The Living Seas
by Frances Dipper and Tony Woodward

Sketchbook Arabia
by Margaret Henderson

The Thesiger Collection
a catalogue of photographs
by Wilfred Thesiger

Thesiger's Return
by Peter Clark
with photographs by Wilfred Thesiger

Storm Command
by General Sir Peter de la Billière

This Strange Eventful History
by Edward Henderson

Juha – Last of the Errant Knights
by Mustapha Kamal,
translated by Jack Briggs

Fun in the Emirates
by Aisha Bowers
and Leslie P. Engelland

Mother Without a Mask
by Patricia Holton

Premier Editions

Desert, Marsh and Mountain
by Wilfred Thesiger

A Day Above Oman
by John Nowell

Forts of Oman
by Walter Dinteman

Land of the Emirates
by Shirley Kay

Enchanting Oman
by Shirley Kay

Abu Dhabi – Garden City of the Gulf
edited by Ian Fairservice
and Peter Hellyer

Arabian Heritage Guides

Snorkelling and Diving in Oman
by Rod Salm and Robert Baldwin

The Green Guide to the Emirates
by Marycke Jongbloed

Off-Road in the Emirates
by Dariush Zandi

Off-Road in Oman
by Heiner Klein
and Rebecca Brickson

Spoken Arabic – Step-by-Step
by John Kirkbright

Arabian Albums

Dubai – An Arabian Album
by Ronald Codrai

Abu Dhabi – An Arabian Album
by Ronald Codrai

MOTIVATE
PUBLISHING